ECOWOMANISM

Ecology and Justice

An Orbis Series on Integral Ecology

Advisory Board Members
Mary Evelyn Tucker
John A. Grim
Leonardo Boff
Sean McDonagh

The Orbis Series on Integral Ecology publishes books seeking to integrate an understanding of Earth's interconnected life systems with sustainable social, political, and economic systems that enhance the Earth community. Books in the series concentrate on ways to

- Reexamine human–Earth relations in light of contemporary cosmological and ecological science.
- Develop visions of common life marked by ecological integrity and social justice.
- Expand on the work of those exploring such fields as integral ecology, climate justice, Earth law, ecofeminism, and animal protection.
- Promote inclusive participatory strategies that enhance the struggle of Earth's poor and oppressed for ecological justice.
- Deepen appreciation for dialogue within and among religious traditions on issues of ecology and justice.
- Encourage spiritual discipline, social engagement, and the transformation of religion and society toward these ends.

Viewing the present moment as a time for fresh creativity and inspired by the encyclical *Laudato Si'*, the series seeks authors who speak to ecojustice concerns and who bring into this dialogue perspectives from the Christian communities, from the world's religions, from secular and scientific circles, or from new paradigms of thought and action.

ECOWOMANISM

African American Women and Earth-Honoring Faiths

by

MELANIE L. HARRIS

ORBIS BOOKS
www.orbisbooks.com

ORBIS BOOKS
Maryknoll, New York 10545

Fathers and Brothers
MARYKNOLL ™

Founded in 1970, Orbis Books endeavors to publish works that enlighten the mind, nourish the spirit, and challenge the conscience. The publishing arm of the Maryknoll Fathers and Brothers, Orbis seeks to explore the global dimensions of the Christian faith and mission, to invite dialogue with diverse cultures and religious traditions, and to serve the cause of reconciliation and peace. The books published reflect the views of their authors and do not represent the official position of the Maryknoll Society. To learn more about Maryknoll and Orbis Books, please visit our website at www.maryknollsociety.org.

Library of Congress Cataloging-in-Publication Data

Names: Harris, Melanie L., 1975– author.
Title: Ecowomanism : African American women and earth-honoring faiths / by Melanie L. Harris.
Description: Maryknoll : Orbis Books, 2017. | Series: Ecology and justice, an Orbis series on integral ecology | Includes bibliographical references and index.
Identifiers: LCCN 2017007217 (print) | LCCN 2017026684 (ebook) | ISBN 9781608336661 (e-book) | ISBN 9781626982017 (pbk.)
Subjects: LCSH: African American women—Religion. | Womanist theology—United States. | Womanism—United States. | Ecotheology—United States. | Aesthetics—Religious aspects.
Classification: LCC BL2525 (ebook) | LCC BL2525 .H365 2017 (print) | DDC 202.082—dc23
LC record available at https://lccn.loc.gov/2017007217

In memory of

my father

John Arberia Harris Sr.

In love for

my mother

Rev. Dr. Naomi O. Harris

and my brother

John Jay Arberia Harris Jr.

and my loving family

Contents

Acknowledgments

Honoring the earth is the hope of this book. The plenty in these pages would not be complete without acknowledging the gifts of water and spirit, earth, air, and energy. I am also grateful for the art of writing and the friends who have accompanied me on this journey. I would like to thank my mother, Rev. Dr. Naomi O. Harris, for her wisdom, love, and insight into the sacred path that has led me to environmental justice. It is her cherishing of the planet that encouraged me to start asking important earth justice sustainability questions early in life. My brother, John Jay Arberia Harris Jr., encouraged and supported me since we were both children enjoying peace, laughter, and fulfilling work in the Colorado sun. I am grateful for a friend and champion on the journey. I give thanks for the gift of the ancestral connection with my father, John Arberia Harris Sr. Daddy, I love you.

The gift of family love has grown through the writing of this book. I would like to thank Molly Harris; Emersyn Grace Harris; Sonia Denise, Keith, Alisha, Nathan, and Desmond Dozier; Clara Beauman; Hattie Patterson; Premilee Reed Turner; and the Harris, Jones, Jiles, and Perry families for being love embodied. I have been blessed with a wonderful spiritual mother in Alice Walker whose presence as guide, justice keeper, and wise and open heart has helped me grow in the light of hope—always. Mama Alice, thank you for loving me. I give thanks for your earth-honoring faith, your awak-ened heart, and your enlightened mind that opens worlds of light to so many.

Friendship like water has nurtured me through the process of writing this book. I honor this as healing grace and peace in my life. I am grateful to my dear friends and sisters Kate Ott, Jennifer Harvey, Carolyn Medine, Monica Maher, Joretta Marshall, Joy Allen, Emilie M. Townes, Laurel Snieder, Rachel E. Harding, Felita Johnson, Cynthia Moe-Lobeda, Layli Maparyan, Stacie McCormick, Fran Huckaby, Claire Sanders, Helen Rhee, Kim-berly Patton, Nisha Botchwey, and Cheryl Walker, who have helped me to breathe deep, show up, take notice, pray, and be present. Spiritual friends and companions have helped sustain me. I would like to thank Lee Self, Lori Hartmann, Brandon Johnson, Chris Patterson, Stephanie Crumpton, Eboni Mar-shall Turman, Keri Day, Danielle Ayers, Patricia Raybon, Wil Gafney, Matthew Williams, James Logan, Josef Sorett, Brian Ott Hill, Jonathan Harding, Jonathan Walton, Willie Jennings, and Ralph Watkins for holding me accountable to joy and excellence in scholarship and writing.

For the sheer gift of a healthy, loving faith community com-mitted to social justice and the beloved community, I would like thank Rev. Dr. Frederick Douglass Haynes and the family of Friendship West Baptist Church and the G.A.A.P. commu-nity. Pastor Haynes, you are a dear brother, scholar, and global pastor in the work of justice, and I am grateful to you and your family for spiritual care, profound writing, and leader-ship. Thank you and Debra Peek Haynes for sharing your faith with so many. Rev. Dr. James Forbes and Mrs. Betty Forbes have continued to be rocks of empowerment and spiritual guides for me. Thank you. I would also like to thank Rev. Talitha Arnold and the United Church of Santa Fe, the Spirit Lake Sisters, and Courage for Care. The GreenFaith commu-nity and brilliant leadership of Fletcher Harper and Stacey Kennealy helped to make this book possible. I would also like to thank the Samuel DeWitt Proctor Conference, Iliff School of Theology, Ghost Ranch Earth Honoring Faith Seminars, the Ford Foundation, the Forum for Theological Exploration, the American Academy of Religion, the Wabash Center for Teaching and Learning in Theology and Religion, and Lilly Endowment Inc. for research funding and teaching opportunities to deepen this work.

Mentors and guides in the fields of womanist religious thought and environmental ethics have helped shape my scholarship. I would like to thank the Womanist Compassion and Justice Consultation groups at the Center for World Religions at Harvard University, Charles Hallisey, Janet Gyatso, and Frank Clooney for the incredible intellectual community we've been able to build together. And I also thank Delores S. Williams, Katie G. Cannon, Marcia Y. Riggs, Rebecca Chopp, Frank Tuitt, Gloria Steinem, Kwok Pui Lan, Shannon Clarkson, Larry and Nyla Rasmussen, Willie Jennings, Norman Wirzba, Willis Jenkins, Mercy Oduyoye, Sofia Betancourt, Xiumei Pu, Rose Mary Emenga-Etego, Valdina Oliveria Pinto, John Makransky, Julia Forsyth, Brooke Lavelle, Mary Evelyn Tucker, John Grim, and Christopher Key Chapple for inviting me to join the discourse of religion and ecology in new ways.

Teaching and research mutually enhance each other. I am grateful to the students whom I have had the privilege of working with in learning communities at Texas Christian University (TCU), Union Theological Seminary in New York City, Iliff School of Theology, Duke Divinity School, Harvard Divinity School, Spelman College, Southern Methodist University, and Methodist Theological School in Ohio, and throughout the world in teaching seminars and lectures featuring ecowomanism.

Faculty, staff, and administrators at TCU have helped support my teaching, research, academic service, and professional leadership development for many years. I would like to thank Chancellor Victor J. Boschini, Provost Nowell Donovan, and Chief Inclusiveness Officer Dr. Darron Turner for their support of African American and Africana Studies at TCU. The Religion Department at TCU has offered a space for me to teach my scholarship. I am grateful for the tradition of good teaching in this context.

Finally I would like to thank Jim Keane, Robert Ellsberg, Elisabeth Begley, and the Maryknoll Mission Institute for their support of this book and the opportunity to share it with you, the reader, a new friend on the journey.

In Peace and Thanksgiving,
Dr. Melanie L. Harris

CHAPTER ONE

Honoring Ecowomanist Experience

My mother's gardens bloom full of flowers most of the year. She is a native of Mississippi and the seventh child of twelve. Her own mother, Bessie Helen Wells, was a teacher and a farmer's daughter. Alexander Spears, my great-grandfather, believed in communing with the earth. This is why the seven daughters and sons whom he and my great-grandmother Martha Spears raised were expected to know how to feed hogs, raise chickens, and grow grain. She was given what I now call an agricultural epistemology that was spiritual in orientation. She was not only taught to feed, raise, and grow, but to nurture, love, and respect every aspect of earth.

There are many stories of how my grandmother learned to read. Some say she practiced on almost everybody she knew. When they grew tired or impatient, she withdrew to the farm. I imagine her, book in hand, reading out loud to chickens and practicing her pronunciation in the ears of horses. It is no wonder that when I came along, it was normal for my own mother, Naomi, to teach me that the best way to grow plants, beans, and flowers was to read to them, and sing. "Sing?" I would always ask. "Yes, sing," my mother would say, and then she would show me how to hum and pray while the flowers drank from the watering can.

Perhaps the greatest songs I've ever heard sung in the garden were African American spirituals, which made me feel a divine ancestral presence all around. Floating freely in the divine tones of music coming from within my own soul, I danced from flowerbed to flowerbed, admiring and singing the spirituals and sacred slave songs I learned in church. Gazing at bees already humming at my mother's roses, I noticed that we all seem to be singing the same song. Even the color of the roses added a melodic tune. Listening is a core part of singing. I learned this early, and the more I listened the louder the music of the earth grew.

Every May in Colorado, as summer blooms, the song that rises most is the one from the wild roses in my mother's garden. It is a secret song at first, and by summer's end, it blooms into a symphony. Inch by inch, foot by foot, the strong green branches of the rosebush stretch up, encouraged by the length of the aspen tree that stands beside it. Knowing their own beauty, and sharing space with the aspen roots, the roses come to full voice, bursting out when aspens bloom with roses. The green leaf tip of aspen appears to open into a deep pink fully petaled rose. The bloom reaches up to the blue sky, itself seemingly endless, and the sky itself seems to take the form of yet another bloom awakening. The song is worth witnessing every year—and each time, as beautiful as a pure human voice is, I fall in love again with the sweet silence and reverence of the beauty of earth, when roses sing with aspens.

Earth Story:
An Ecowomanist Ecoautobiography

Embodied with a deep mystical connection to African, African American, and Native American ancestors, I find it easy to feel at home in the West and Southwest. The landscape of

the Rocky Mountains is home to me. It is here where my personal journey into environmental awareness begins, rooted in
the ancient presence of the tall mountains surrounding Den-
ver and in the loving home where I lived with my immediate
family: my brother, "Jay" John A. Harris Jr., and my parents,
Naomi O. Harris and John A. Harris Sr. The lineage of earth-
honoring faith on my father's side began many generations
before I arrived. My grandfather Singleton Harris and my
grandmother Lucy Harris were among the millions of *black
environmentalists* who left the terror of Jim Crow in the South
with the waves of the Great Migration and traveled west.
Leaving behind prayerful arms of protection from family in
Mississippi, my father's parents were among the first black
settlers to start new life in Dearfield, Colorado. Knowing deep
within themselves that the Cherokee and Mississippi Blackfoot
ancestral echoes in their souls were somehow connected to the
rocky and desertlike soil they met in Colorado, my grandparents, I believe, took heart as they, like millions of other black
families, began to plant hope for new beginnings in the hard
earth with their blood, sweat, and tears.

I am also part white, a result of the sexual violence forced
on black enslaved women by white male slave owners in the
South. This is a very important aspect of African and African
American family history and trauma. It is also an important
aspect of the history of race in America, though it is rarely
acknowledged or talked about. What is significant for ecowomanism is that this violent part of racial history in the
United States has a deep impact on the environmental history
of this space as well.

While it is more complicated to rationalize the sense of
home that I also feel when I return to the dark woods of Mississippi, it is often there in the bosom of family, and the safety
of collective memory of song and hope, that I continue to
find strength in the face of fighting the structural evil of white
supremacy; and I remain loyal to the hard work of staying
attentive and being aware of the logic of domination that is

surely at play in the history of lynching in this country, the legacy of Jim Crow, and the rising numbers of unjust killings of black men and black women in order to terrorize black communities into a constant state of fear. Regardless of the struggle for freedom in the South, I, too, call Mississippi home.[1]

I call this sense of home a part of an ecowomanist paradigm that helps African peoples recover and reclaim their connection to earth and their relationship with the land. This act of ecomemory, a concept discussed in Chapter Two, is also an act of political resistance. It insists that the metanarrative of environmental history is ill informed and malformed in part because it does not include (and sometimes denies) the histories, presence, and contributions of peoples of color, including Native Americans and African Americans, to the environmental movement. In this sense, the recovery of African American environmental history is key not only to correcting the lens of environmental history, but also to establishing the roots of African American environmental religious history and ecowomanism more firmly.

As one might imagine, this history is complex and not without paradox. In fact, a *beauty-to-burden* paradox is woven throughout most of African American environmental history, and this frame is important to acknowledge for the sake of establishing African American ecomemory and tracing the inheritance of African American environmental history. This concept was coined by ecoliterary writer Kimberly Ruffin in her book *Black on Earth: African American Ecoliterary Traditions*[2] and attempts to explain how the gulf between the horrors of lynching as part of a black southern *connection* to nature is bridged with the spiritual intimacy that many descendants of Africa have with the earth today.[3] According to historian Isabel

---

[1] Of particular resonance for me here is Nina Simone, "Mississippi Goddam," on *A Single Woman*, Elektra, 2008, CD.

[2] Kimberly N. Ruffin, *Black on Earth: African American Ecoliterary Traditions* (Athens: University of Georgia Press, 2010).

[3] For more on Alice Walker's sense of home, see my analysis of her

Wilkerson, the author of *The Warmth of Other Suns: The Epic Story of America's Great Migration,*[4] many of these descendants are in fact going back to the South for this same sense of home. In what is known as the *new great migration*, African Americans from urban areas across the United States are returning to the South. After six decades of African Americans leaving the South between 1914 and 1970, now more and more African Americans are returning to the South for a connection to rural life—a chance to touch the earth. From an ecowomanist perspective, this move signals not only a desire for peoples to experience a slower pace and simpler lifestyle, but also a desire to reconnect with nature and return to black nature.

Before the writings of Ruffin and Wilkerson, there were other theorists, writers, poets, and historians writing about this same aspect of home and African Americans' connection to the earth. Alice Walker, literary artist and Pulitzer Prize–winning author of *The Color Purple,* has written extensively about African Americans' connection to the earth and is heralded as one of the pioneering ecowomanist thinkers and scholars. Her essay "The Only Reason You Want to Go to Heaven,"[5] "Choice: A Tribute to Dr. Martin Luther King, Jr.,"[6] as well as her nonfiction essays about Coretta Scott King and her poetry, are brilliant examples of ecowomanist thought and African American environmental history. As I have written elsewhere, Walker's reflection on her own home of Eatonton, Georgia,

nonfiction essays in Melanie L. Harris, *Gifts of Virtue, Alice Walker, and Womanist Ethics* (New York: Palgrave Macmillan, 2010), 17.

[4] Isabel Wilkerson, *The Warmth of Other Suns: The Epic Story of America's Great Migration* (New York: Vintage, 2011).

[5] Alice Walker, "The Only Reason You Want to Go to Heaven Is That You Have Been Driven Out of Your Mind (Off Your Land and Out of Your Lover's Arms): Clear Seeing Inherited Religion and Reclaiming the Pagan Self," in *Anything We Love Can Be Saved: A Writer's Activism* (New York: Random House, 1997), 3–27.

[6] Alice Walker, "Choice: A Tribute to Dr. Martin Luther King, Jr.," in *In Search of Our Mothers' Gardens: Womanist Prose* (New York: Harcourt Brace and Jovanovich, 1983), 163.

is particularly helpful in establishing a method for ecowomanist thought. Her writings also provide examples of African American activist presence in the environmental movement. In *Gifts of Virtue, Alice Walker, and Womanist Ethics*, I summarize some of the values that arise from Walker's ecowomanist ethics from writings about her family home.

> For more than one hundred years, the Walker family has called Eatonton home. Claiming this title based on her ancestors' spiritual and physical connection to the land as sharecroppers and former slaves, Walker explains that while the racist laws of the segregated south prohibited her family from owning the land they worked and tilled for generations, the grave markers that serve as a final resting place for her loved ones are the proof that "the land of my birthplace belongs to me, dozens of times over." . . . This move to reclaim birthplace and reestablish home are major themes in Walker's writings and surface as significant values expressed throughout her non-fiction work. She writes extensively about the values of belonging, having a place to call one's own and home in relation to the pain of black peoples' agony of having been ripped from their ancestral land of Africa, and the sheer strength and courage it took to build a place for themselves in the United States. . . . Being forced to work the land, and also holding deep respect for the land and its rich resources for health and well-being presented a tension [paradox] within the story of African people's connection to the earth, and relationship with land.[7]

Regarding Alice Walker's own ecowomanist sensibilities, and her awareness of African American environmental history from within her own family, I present the following analysis:

---

[7] Harris, *Gifts of Virtue, Alice Walker, and Womanist Ethics*, 17.

The sense of belonging to place, and the important history of owning and having land taken away from the Walker family based on their race is important to uncovering Alice Walker's spiritual value of the earth, and creates an opening through which to understand the important sense of belonging and home connected to place and community in her thinking.[8]

Following a methodological process of uncovering one's own environmental familial roots and spiritual connections, the first step of an ecowomanist method begins with investigating one's family story and connection with the earth. This is modeled in Walker's writings and serves as an important model for ecowomanist method. I continue in this vein in the next section, honoring the earth story of both sides of my family lineage and my own ecowomanist experience before moving into an outline of the remainder of the book.

A Family Ecojourney

My paternal grandparents came to the Rocky Mountains ready to work with the land. They came from Mississippi, a place of rich, deep, fertile soil and a seemingly even deeper history of white supremacy and violence against black people. Seeing lynched bodies hanging from southern trees was a common sight when my grandmother was young, and there was always a tale or two about just why white southerners hated black people so much. According to my grandmother's Christian theology, the hate received was not to be returned, but rather transformed through love.[9] And perhaps it was because she had practiced love so deeply that she felt so powerfully drawn to another place, a place where she could experience love more

---

[8] Ibid.

[9] For a deeper understanding of the feel and tone of this theology, listen to "Prayer," by Sweet Honey in the Rock, comp. Ysaye Barnwell, *Sacred Ground*, Earthbeat, 1995, CD.

fully, share health and well-being with her family, and finally live freely. Or perhaps it was because she was so in love with my grandfather and was willing to risk so much, leaving her well-to-do, fair-skinned, black, Blackfoot, and Cherokee blood family line and come out west—to plant, to grow, to love. This love story always intrigues me.

Full of courage, my grandparents arrived in Colorado following the birth of the first black settlement (also called a black agricultural colony) in the state, Dearfield. Founded in 1910 by O. T. Jackson and named for the cherished sentiment the black people who lived there held for the land, 160 acres of land was transformed into a community within the first five years.[10] In 1910, the first seven families moved to Dearfield, living in tents and dugouts. By 1911, two frame houses were built, allowing the families to survive the severe winter. By 1915, a community was established. Twenty-seven families now lived in forty-four wood cabins, and they built a grocery store, a concrete block factory, a dance pavilion, a lodge, a restaurant, and a boardinghouse. With the brave help, back-breaking labor, prayer, sweat, and tears of the black women and black men, including my grandparents, these settlers dry farmed corn, oats, barley, alfalfa, hay, potatoes, Mexican beans, sugar beets, cantaloupes, strawberries, and more. They made Dearfield their home. They also made history. Dearfield is still known today as one of the first and most successful black-owned settlements in the United States.

They were not alone.

During the Great Migration, over the course of six decades more than six million black people left the South for a better life, a more just space, and better job opportunities. As Wilkerson's book brilliantly tells the story, people left in droves to board buses, trains, automobiles, and buggies to escape the air of the rural South filled with the scent of lynching, the

---

[10] While there is much information about Dearfield in online sources, to date there are not many book-length volumes published on its history. For some of the best online sources of information, see http://www.unco.edu.

impossible-to-profit system of sharecropping, and the all too real remnants of slavery.[11] They left places like Louisiana and Alabama for Detroit and Chicago. More left the banks of the Mississippi for New York and Baltimore. Between 1910 and 1971, millions showed up on the doorsteps of new possibility in the North, Midwest, and West.

The first wave came between 1910 and 1930, with the hearts of 1.6 million. Hundreds of thousands followed during World War II; more still came in the decades following. This constant flow of people topped the numbers of humans worldwide who have ever moved willingly from one place to another in such a short period of time. By its end, the Great Migration was one of the most significant episodes of American history, whereby millions of Americans left the terrorist normalcy of the racial injustice of the Jim Crow South for a new life. Like my grandparents, they came with hope in their hearts, an oaklike strength, and determination to work hard. Their courage created a wave of cultural power in the United States and reshaped the life and identity of America.

Overview of This Book

This book tells the story of one aspect of African American environmental history from a womanist perspective. More specifically, it engages womanist religious thought and uses a womanist methodological lens to illumine how important African and African American women's voices are to the work of environmental justice. *Ecowomanism* signals the importance of developing an interdisciplinary approach and method to doing environmental justice work. From my perspective, this includes the disciplines of religion, culture, and ethics but also points to the significant influence that the disciplines of literature, sociology, geography, critical race theory, and feminist and womanist thought have made to wider conversations about climate change.

---

[11] Wilkerson, *The Warmth of Other Suns.*

Born from a liberationist theological frame, the steps of this book's presentation follow an ecowomanist methodological path.[12] Ecowomanist method is not linear, but rather follows a spiral-like pattern where steps are interchangeable. The analysis from one step dovetails and expands the analysis from and for another step.

Beginning with a focus on honoring ecowomanist experience, I first reveal my own ecowomanist ecoautobiography and share the story of my entry into the environmental justice movement. The next methodological step is to reflect on this experience using multiple tools of analysis. This process takes shape in Chapter Two and is echoed throughout the chapters that follow. One of the tools used to reflect on the experience is womanist social analysis. By using a race–class–gender analytical lens from which to examine the ecowomanist experience, this step, discussed in Chapter Two, can provide new perspectives on the ecological crisis we are living in. This chapter also clearly explicates the seven-step ecowomanist method.

After Chapter Two has explicated the method fully and illustrated the first three steps, Chapter Three features step four of the method, critically examining African and African American history and tradition. Prompted by the previous analysis in steps two and three, and in order to uncover more accurate accounts of African American environmental history and uncover religious heritages, this step focuses on contributions helpful for building an ecowomanist ethic.

Next I examine this history and tradition by closely looking at the parallel examples of the *sin of defilement* that devalues the lives and bodies of black women and the body of the earth. Here, ecowomanist analysis helps to examine the intersecting nature of oppressions that work to undermine wholeness in the self as well as planetary wholeness. Building on womanist

---

[12] This is explained in Chapter Two. Ecowomanist methodology is influenced by black liberationist as well as womanist and feminist approaches to the study and practice of religion.

social analysis, which insists that multilayered oppressions be exposed, this chapter concludes by introducing ecowomanist spirituality as a response to the environmental crisis we are living in today.

Chapter Four focuses on ecowomanist spirituality as praxis and follows the methodological step five of engaging transformation. This chapter is unique in that it features the work of three ecowomanist scholars and the models of ecowomanist spirituality that flow from their writings. As such, the chapter uncovers an ecowomanist moral landscape that is diasporic in scope and interreligious in nature.

This interreligious aspect of ecowomanism is discussed in Chapter Five. One of the most important contributions of ecowomanism is its approach to interfaith and interreligious issues as well as its emphasis on comparative theological discourse. This methodological step honors the process of shared dialogue with multiple religious earth-honoring faith traditions that also honor African and African American women's ecowomanist spirituality.

Expanding on this dialogue, Chapter Six turns to step seven of an ecowomanist method: taking action for earth justice through teaching ecowomanism. This chapter features pedagogical strategies on how to teach an ecowomanist method in academic, church, and community classrooms, and the important impact this can have on raising awareness about the ethical, moral mandate to care for the earth and honor the interconnectedness of life.

Chapter Seven closes the book with important analysis of the scholarly and praxis contributions that the Black Lives Matter movement makes to environmental justice. This is important as we engage in global conversations about the impact of climate change on communities of color and the disproportionate ways environmental health hazards impact these communities more negatively than white and European communities. African and African American women's earth-honoring faiths are vital to the growth, theorizing, and practice of environmental justice. This book provides a method for helping us all move in that direction.

The book is also a narrative of my own ecoautobiography, which helps to set the context for ecowomanism and reveals the crucial voices and spiritual activism of African American women who have been involved in the environmental justice movement for decades. By tracing the story of my grandparents, who left Mississippi with the Great Migration and moved out West, I show how their ecomemory and ethical value to care for the earth was woven into a deep commitment to freedom and was a part of the practice of their Christian spirituality. This same ethical mandate to cherish the earth as a part of one's religious duty and to honor the earth through one's spiritual life was passed down from my grandparents. It lives on now in the religious and spiritual lives of my family, which is recorded in this book for future generations.

CHAPTER TWO

Ecowomanism 101: Method and Approaches

The previous chapter began to explore the origins of ecowomanism. It opened up the discourse that reveals an ecowomanist story, prompting us to honor ecowomanist experience before diving into the second and third methodological steps of reflecting on that experience and using womanist intersectional analysis as a part of that reflection. This chapter explicates those two steps and conducts analysis of the historical experiences of women of African descent—their cosmologies, spiritual truths, and religiosities that shape new perspectives on earth justice.[1] Before moving into this formal analysis,

---

[1] I would like to thank the American Academy of Religion's Womanist Approaches to Religion and Society section for accepting a paper that served as a foundation for this chapter. I would also like to thank Dr. Melinda Berry and partners with GreenFaith, Rev. Fletcher Harper, and Earth Honoring Faith and the Religions for the Earth Conference in advance of the UN Climate Change Meeting in New York in 2015 for the comments, contributions, and feedback offered on initial versions of this chapter.

however, it is helpful to illustrate each of the methodological steps of ecowomanism and then explain how ecowomanism gives attention to theory and praxis.

Ecowomanism: Theory and Praxis

Ecowomanist approaches can be described as the reflective and contemplative study of the ecowisdom that is theorized, constructed, and practiced by women of African descent. The discourse validates their lives, spiritual values, and activism as important epistemologies (i.e., sets of knowledge) in ecowomanism. As with most discourses emerging from womanist thought, ecowomanist theory is shaped by critical study and observation of praxis and vice versa. That is, womanist ethical theory is shaped by careful, critical reflection and study of the practice of ethical mores, behaviors, and actions within African and African American communities. Some authors, including Peter J. Paris, argue that such study reveals a connection between the moral landscapes in all communities across the African diaspora. In his work *The Spirituality of African Peoples: The Search for a Common Moral Landscape*,[2] he argues that all African communities share common ethical values such as community, liberation, and honoring the ancestors. Using a virtue ethical approach, Paris sifts through these values and others to articulate a set of virtues that summarize an ethical system. These virtues include beneficence, forbearance, practical wisdom, improvisation, forgiveness, and justice.

One of the most significant contributions of Paris's scholarship is his reference to the African cosmology that shapes the moral, ethical worldview of many African peoples and communities. Spirit, nature, and humanity are connected in an interdependent web of life in African cosmology. Thus, any ethical or unethical behavior conducted by humans impacts

---

[2] Peter J. Paris, *The Spirituality of African Peoples: The Search for a Common Moral Landscape* (Minneapolis: Fortress Press, 1995).

the other aspects of the cosmological order positively or negatively. According to this framework, one could argue that since ancestors are believed to reside in many aspects of nature, any human behavior that diminishes and dishonors nature or the earth can have a devastating impact on the relationship between the human and the ancestor. In the case of water pollution, for example, the act of humans misusing, damaging, wasting, or abusing water is understood to be an immoral act against nature, which disrespects the ancestors. In this sense, the common ethical worldview that Paris describes has woven within it an ethical mandate to care for the earth. This important ethical frame for earth justice also can be said to be innate to African and African American life; thus, an ethical mandate to care for the earth is considered normative in many African cultures and communities.[3]

As I have argued in earlier work,[4] this African cosmological vision provides a base from which an ethical mandate for earth justice can be gleaned. This is, of course, one of the focal points of ecowomanism.

Womanist theory and praxis go hand in hand. In the same way that womanist theory is shaped by careful observation and study of praxis, so, too, is the praxis shaped by the theory.

---

[3] It is important to note how the work of Jacob Olupona, Edward P. Antonio, and other African religion scholars have contributed and critiqued the argument claiming that it universalizes African life and pays little attention to the vast differences and distinctions within African tribes and cultures. These are important critiques in part because of the tendency for colonial ecological arguments to emerge from a theoretical frame that universalizes African traditions and ethics. For more, see Edward P. Antonio, "Ecology as Experience in African Indigenous Religions," in *Living Stones in the Household of God: The Legacy and Future of Black Theology*, ed. Linda E. Thomas, 146–57 (Minneapolis: Fortress Press, 2003).

[4] Melanie L. Harris, "An Ecowomanist Vision," in *Ethics That Matters: African, Caribbean, and African American Sources*, ed. James Logan and Marcia Y. Riggs, 189–93 (Minneapolis: Fortress Press, 2012).

When engaging the practice of building community and deter-mining values that would enhance the lives and communities of African American peoples battling against legalized racial segregation and the brutalities of Jim and Jane Crow, those working to determine practical action regularly engaged with theory. For example, the theory of racial uplift articulated by W. E. B. Du Bois[5] influenced the praxis and activism of civic empowerment organizations such as the National Association of Colored Women's Clubs. In keeping with (and expanding) the theory of racial uplift, this organization adopted the motto *lift as we climb*. It was led by some of the most renowned African American women educators, community leaders, and civil rights activists of the nineteenth century; women including Harriet Tubman, Frances E. W. Harper, Josephine St. Pierre Ruffin, Margaret Murray Washington, Ida B. Wells-Barnett, and Mary Church Terrell (the organization's first president) helped shape a praxis-oriented ethic that guided African American communities into liberation.[6] Emerging from womanist thought, then, ecowomanism embodies both theory and praxis.

Critical Reflection on Experience and Womanist Intersectional Analysis: Deconstructive and Constructive

Another mark of womanist liberationist thought that ecowom-anism embodies is an emphasis on critical deconstructive analysis and the development of a constructive approach. For woman-ists, it is not enough to interrogate and deconstruct structures of oppression; it is also necessary to work for the construction of corrective models, methods that debunk racialized myths and stereotypes, and approaches that are liberating for all of

---

[5] W. E. B. Du Bois, *Souls of Black Folk*, unabridged version (New York: Dover Publications, 1994).

[6] See http://www.pbs.org/wnet/jimcrow/stories_org_nacw.html.

the earth community. Womanist ethicist Marcia Y. Riggs captures this constructive task of womanist ethical discourse, noting that the womanist project seeks to engage in several tasks, including "constructing black womanist theology and religious ethics in light of the first two tasks [uncover womanist roots and debunk social myths about women of African descent] and to broaden these disciplines to include nontraditional bases and sources for theological and ethical reflection."[7]

Because of its focus on environmental justice, ecowomanism offers a critical deconstructive analytical approach to systems of colonial ecology. Using a deconstructive lens, ecowomanism critiques environmental approaches that ignore the history of environmental justice work, which is historically led by communities of color, and refuses to acknowledge the impact of white supremacy on the development of the current environmental movement. For example, while climate change will have a devastating impact on the entire planet, it is already having an impact on communities of color that suffer most from climate variations but often contribute the least to it. As environmental ethicist Cynthia Moe-Lobeda observes in her book *Resisting Structural Evil: Love as Ecological-Economic Vocation*, it is crucial to examine the links between climate violence, white privilege, the historical impact of white supremacy in the United States and globally, and an environmentally exploitive capitalist paradigm.[8]

Critical Deconstructive Analysis

The primary deconstructive analytical approach used in ecowomanism is womanist and black feminist race–class–gender analysis. This analysis raises important questions

---

[7] Marcia Y. Riggs, *Awake, Arise and Act: A Womanist Call for Black Liberation* (Cleveland, OH: Pilgrim Press, 1994), 2.

[8] Cynthia Moe-Lobeda, *Resisting Structural Evil: Love as Ecological-Economic Vision* (Minneapolis: Fortress Press, 2013).

about how racism and the history of white supremacy may impact environmental policy, perspective, and understanding; how assumptions about economic class privilege might shape environmental outlook; and how and why it is important to examine how gendering the earth as mother opens up a gender critique as the logic of domination that subdues the feminine in the culture is revealed. A focus on gender in ecowomanist analysis is paradoxical in that it simultaneously uncovers an innate solidarity between women and the earth. This solidarity is especially important in the work of ecowomanism, since it draws parallels between the way that enslaved African women's bodies were violated, raped, and abused by white oppressors functioning according to the logic of domination, and the way the body of the earth feminine has been abused at the hands of its abusers. The critical deconstructive analysis featured in ecowomanist thought reveals the systemic nature of parallel oppressions that black women and the earth face. However, this analysis also reveals an element of the constructive approach of ecowomanism, namely, the agency-producing and activist-oriented recognition of solidarity between women of color, and particularly women of African descent, and the earth. This will be discussed more in the section featuring the constructive elements of ecowomanism.

Using womanist, black, feminist, race–class–gender analysis as a part of the critical deconstructive aspect of an ecowomanist approach means that ecowomanism "applies womanist intersectional analysis to issues of environmental concern in order to engage the complex ways racism, classism, sexism, and heterosexism operate in situations of environmental injustice."[9] Rather than universalizing human experience with the earth, or basing human-to-earth interactions on the experience of white middle- to upper-class women and men, ecowomanism marks the particularities of the relationship between women of African descent and the earth. Ecowomanism exposes the impact of

---

[9] Harris, "An Ecowomanist Vision," 191–92.

structural racism and systemic oppression assumed in many traditional paths in the environmental movement, and articulates a corrective that shows the connection between social injustice and environmental injustice.

Beyond explaining the basic frames of an ecowomanist approach, it is also important to recognize that the adoption of the womanist black feminist method for ecowomanism establishes an intellectual link to the intellectual lineage of African, Africana, and black thought. Interdisciplinary in its nature, ecowomanism shares basic sources that inform these disciplines of study, as well as the sociopolitical nature and liberating ideology that is historically connected to this heritage. Whether in the writings of Ida B. Wells, the speeches of Sojourner Truth, or the abolitionist activism of Harriet Tubman, the emphasis on political, physical, psychological, spiritual, sexual, and economic freedom of African peoples and their communities is woven into an emphasis on freedom of environmental health and wholeness in ecowomanist thought.[10]

Since ecowomanism connects a political, liberationist, theological, and religio-spiritual social justice agenda with earth justice, by its nature, it engages an interdisciplinary conversation. That is, while deeply influenced by the disciplines of womanist and black feminist ethics, religion and ecology, and spiritual ecology, ecowomanism uses interdisciplinary approaches that combine resources and methods from fields such as environmental studies, ethics, sociology, religion, anthropology, agricultural studies, history, geology, health and medicine, and more.[11] While many interdisciplinary methods

---

[10] Some may argue that this is unabashedly anthropocentric. My response to this, similar to Katie G. Cannon's, is that ecowomanism is unapologetically for the liberation of African peoples and the wholeness of the earth community.

[11] For more on the precedent for the use of interdisciplinary methodology in womanist religious thought, see my analysis of the scholarly method of Katie G. Cannon in Melanie L. Harris, *Gifts of Virtue, Alice*

inform ecowomanist method, perhaps the most primary analytical frame that is often highlighted in womanist thought is a race–class–gender analysis.

Constructive Approaches

Methodologically, ecowomanist approaches use womanist black feminist race–class–gender analysis that consistently looks through a lens that exposes tripartite oppressions imposed by systems of white supremacy and racial privilege that attempt to negate the lives, innate worth, value, and dignity of black women and communities of color. Even as ecowomanism attempts to dismantle or disrupt systems of oppression and realities of climate violence, traditional womanist black feminist method is also constructive. It highlights strategies of resistance, spiritual resilience, and intellectual genius solutions for survival that emerge from black women's lives and moral integrity, and directly addresses climate justice. Ecowomanism, then, offers unique gifts to the environmental activist movement by highlighting the contributions that women of African descent make to the environmental justice movement. As it is influenced by the discipline of religion, and the discourse of spiritual ecology, ecowomanism is also constructive in that it reveals the theological voices and ethical perspectives from women of African descent as they contribute new strategies for facing climate change and promoting earth justice within and beyond faith communities.

Noting the specific historical relationship that African American women have had with the earth (i.e., being named as property the same as the earth and devalued in similar ways as the earth) in the midst of surviving a white supremacist society, ecowomanism pays attention to the complex subjectivity and genius of African American women.

Walker, and Womanist Ethics (New York: Palgrave Macmillan, 2010).

Method, Roots, and Womanist Lineage

In order to even more deeply understand ecowomanist method, it is helpful to make an additional turn into the work and scholarship of Katie G. Cannon. This ethicist is known as a pioneer in womanist ethics, specifically, and womanist religious thought more broadly. While the term *womanist* was coined by Alice Walker and the discourse was already under way in the field of literature, it was Cannon's first published articulation of black feminist consciousness and a womanist ethical approach that opened the doors for womanist ethical and theological discourse to begin. In her essay "The Emergence of Black Feminist Consciousness," she wrote,

> The feminist consciousness of Afro-American women cannot be understood and explained adequately apart from the historical context in which Black women have found themselves as moral agents. . . . Throughout the history of the United States, the interrelationship of White supremacy and male superiority has characterized the Black woman's reality as a situation of struggle. . . . Both in informal day-to-day life and in the formal organizations and institutions in society, Black women are still the victims of the aggravated inequities of the tridimensional phenomenon of race/class/gender oppression. This is the backdrop of the historical context for the emergence of the Black feminist consciousness. . . . [This] may be more accurately identified as Black womanist consciousness, to use Alice Walker's concept and definition.[12]

---

[12] Katie G. Cannon, "The Emergence of Black Feminist Consciousness," in *Katie's Cannon: Womanism and the Soul of the Black Community* (New York: Continuum, 1998), 47–56.

As I have articulated in some of my previous work, the recognition of Walker's conceptual frame and definition of *womanist* is central to the work, scholarship, and approach of womanist analysis. Walker's fiction is repeatedly cited in the scholarship in womanist religious thought, and increasingly her nonfiction essays, blogs, interviews, and speeches are upheld as central sources for womanist thought that engages social justice, human rights, and environmental justice. Walker's work, method, and approach of lifting up the moral lives, codes, experiences, and stories of black women is central for the work of womanist religious thought. It is especially important for ecowomanism, because Walker's nonfiction writing reflects a moral and spiritual commitment to earth-honoring faith and fluid spirituality practices among African women and women of color. It also provides guidance for conceptual framing of ecowomanist method.

In addition to examining how racism, classism, and sexism are systemic oppressive realities imposed on black women by systems and individuals, womanist analysis also critiques systems of heteropatriarchy that may limit the freedom and full expression of black women's sexuality. Pointing to the history of white supremacist, heteropatriarchal policies that were used to control the reproductive choices and agency of black women, womanist analysis also confronts how heteropatriarchal and capitalist systems attempt to dominate the lives and bodies of black women. As has been documented in the work of Delores S. Williams, ecowomanist analysis builds on the observation of systemic oppression of black women's sexuality and compares this to the oppression and violence suffered by the body of the earth. In essays such as "Everything Is a Human Being" and "Nuclear Madness," Walker uses an ecowomanist frame to point out the eerie similarities between the way the logic of domination has attempted to mutate the bodies, minds, and souls of black women, and the logic of domination at play in cases of environmental injustice.[13] A focus on

---

[13] For more on the definition of environmental injustice framing,

these parallel oppressions is one aspect of ecowomanist study. In fact, the method and approach to ecowomanism (the focus of this chapter) emerges from reflections of this aspect of the discourse. In addition to honoring the biodiversity of the earth, ecowomanism honors the varied and particular experiences of African and African American women as human beings living in the earth community. It follows a seven-step approach that is constructive both in that it shapes a womanist social analysis of the environment and frames a lens through which to view issues of ecological violence and environmental health disparity in an age of climate change.

The Seven-Step Ecowomanist Method

Having established the structural frames for ecowomanist analysis, this section explicates the seven-step ecowomanist method. The pattern for this method is a spiral, where each step is interchangeable with the others, rather than following a linear pattern. Similar to the way that justice serves as an overarching value in womanist thought,[14] a sense of prophetic justice hovers over the theorizing, construction, and practice of ecowomanism. Influenced by the African American intellectual tradition of the black prophetic voice, ecowomanism also carries with it a sense of prophetic justice that speaks truth to power and directly addresses the immorality of racism, classism, sexism, homophobia, xenophobia, transphobia, Islamophobia, ageism, and other forms of discriminatory oppression rooted in fear and hate. The black prophetic wisdom tradition links religious understandings to a social justice agenda. That is, as in black liberation theology, a certain authority is granted to African American

---

see Dorceta E. Taylor, "The Rise of the Environmental Justice Paradigm: Injustice Framing and the Social Construction of Environmental Discourses," *American Behavioral Scientist* 43, no. 4 (2000): 508–80, and Moe-Lobeda, *Resisting Structural Evil*.

[14] Emilie M. Townes, *In a Blaze of Glory: Womanist Spirituality as Social Witness* (Nashville: Abingdon Press, 1995).

hermeneutical readings of the Old Testament. Throughout the Old Testament, a certain pattern is observed in the relationship between God and the people known as God's chosen (the Hebrews) wherein a covenant is established between God and the people, and then the people break the covenant and move away from God's divine teachings. According to the stories, out of God's love, God sends a prophet to correct the people. This prophet's purpose is to remind the people of the covenant, convict them, and guide them back into covenant with God. The steady stream of black prophetic wisdom tradition can be witnessed in such historical leaders as Sojourner Truth, Harriet Tubman, and Frederick Douglass. In each of the speeches or writings of these leaders, one can note the influence of religious truths and the prophetic wisdom tradition woven into a political sense of social justice (i.e., the end of slavery and the full emancipation and reparative support of African enslaved peoples). This same stream of prophetic justice flows through ecowomanism. It also raises social justice concerns of black and African peoples and the rights of communities of color, and also includes a concern for the rights of communities of color to environmental health and safety.

The sense of the prophetic and its connection to environmental justice is perhaps best illustrated in the work of Dr. Martin Luther King Jr., who in April of 1968 came to support a group of sanitation workers in Memphis, Tennessee. As retold by Dianne Glave in her essay "Black Environmental Liberation Theology,"[15] King recognized the courage these workers had to strike as a form of protest, thus exposing the severe inequities that black sanitation workers were facing, the mistreatment they were forced to endure, and the environmental

---

[15] Taylor, "The Rise of the Environmental Justice Paradigm"; Dianne Glave, "Black Environmental Liberation Theology," in Dianne Glave and Mark Stoll, eds., *To Love the Wind and the Rain: African Americans and Environmental History* (Pittsburgh: University of Pittsburgh Press, 2006), 189–99.

health hazards they were forced to contend with in order to keep their jobs. In going to Memphis in 1968, King carefully decided to link the push for civil rights with an awareness of the inequalities resulting from poverty and the lack of environmental health in many poor and African American communities. Memphis sanitation workers were expected to clear trash from rat-infested trash dumps and were exposed to a petri dish of other vermin and insects left swarming around human-made trash heaps. King's intellectual and political move to link social justice civil rights issues to poverty and environmental health set the base for the present-day environmental justice movement, according to Dorceta E. Taylor, Glave, and others.[16] This illustration also shows how King engaged the prophetic wisdom tradition, combining religious oratorical genius with sharp political critique to point out the racial injustice present in Memphis and normative throughout the country. By exposing the structural violence that was based on racism, dehumanization, and exploitation of workers' rights, King shed light on the hypocrisy of many white Americans with power and privilege who were not living up to the democratic covenant: the Constitution of the United States.

Recalling the prophetic tone in the voices of Harriet Tubman, Sojourner Truth, Frederick Douglass, and others helps to establish a sense of the black prophetic wisdom tradition that ecowomanism embodies.[17] The prophetic nature of ecowomanism calls for the hard ethical work that needs to be done to respond to immediate ecological issues like environmental health disparities, climate violence, and climate change. It also recognizes the pattern of systemic or structural violence rooted in theologies and histories that need to be carefully remembered

---

[16] Glave, "Black Environmental Liberation Theology," 189–99.

[17] Frederick Douglass, "What to the Slave Is the Fourth of July?" Independence Day 1852, http://www.freemaninstitute.com/douglass.htm. See also Langston Hughes, "Let America Be American," https://www. poets.org/poetsorg/poem/let-america-be-america-again.

and disrupted in order to act more justly. The work of Moe-Lobeda is once again helpful here. She offers several descriptions of terms, including *structural violence*, that aid in the comprehension of the prophetic nature of ecowomanism. She describes structural violence as referring to "the physical, psychological, spiritual harm that certain groups of people experience as the result of unequal distribution of power and privilege."[18]

Reflective of a religious social ethic and liberation theological strain, the prophetic nature of ecowomanism also leaves room for the Spirit and acknowledges a religious (interreligious and intrareligious), sometimes spiritual or mystical, presence that marks an element of the transcendent in the work of ecowomanist thought and practice. That is, ecowomanism unashamedly acknowledges the Spirit. In so doing, it builds on the reference to the same in the womanist definition coined by Walker; a womanist *loves the Spirit*. Honoring this presence of the cognitive and sometimes noncognitive reality of ecowomanism often places the discourse into the field of spiritual ecology; however, it is important to remember the interdisciplinary function and method of ecowomanism, even while recognizing that the discourse includes a mystical reality that speaks prophetically to the reality of the times.

In addition to the prophetic nature of ecowomanism being illustrated by its inclusion of Spirit, this emphasis also connects ecowomanism to the intellectual lineage of the history of African spirituality, African American mysticism, and certainly African American religious history and faith. Noting again the importance of the link between social justice and divine justice, when it comes to earth justice, ecowomanism weaves into its structure, analysis, and conceptual frame an element that sometimes cannot be explained, but rather has to be experienced through engaging activist or spiritual activist community and activity. The presence of prophetic wisdom and the prophetic

---

[18] Moe-Lobeda, *Resisting Structural Evil*, 72.

Spirit, which gives voice to the speaker, reader, student, and scholar of ecowomanism in an era of the Anthropocene, is an important aspect of the discourse.[19]

Step One:
Honoring Experience and Mining Ecomemory

Experience is as much a part of understanding the prophetic nature and prophetic wisdom of ecowomanism as it is a source for ecowomanism. As such, the first methodological step of an ecowomanist method is honoring experience. By honoring the experience of women of African descent through the sharing of ecostory, recalling or retelling the narratives of women of African descent, and examining these ecomemories as countermemory, an ecowomanist approach begins the first step of exposing the truth and debunking myths and stereotypes about women of African descent, peoples of color, and environmental history. Following both a critical deconstructive and constructive approach, honoring experience both dismantles systems of oppression by exposing the terrorist patterns of white supremacy and simultaneously promotes ecowomanist ways of being and their practice of earth-honoring faiths that resist the exploitation of women, peoples of color, and the earth.

Uncovering the unique herstory of the relationship that African and African American women have had with the earth historically is the first step of an ecowomanist method, namely *honoring experience* or mining ecomemory. This process of remembering African American historical roots in the environmental movement highlights the significance of black women's ecospirituality, earth-honoring faith, or earth spiritual activism, and treats these sources as valid epistemologies for environmental discourse. Gleaning important wisdom and knowledge from these women's faith stories, narratives,

---

[19] Willis Jenkins, *The Future of Ethics: Sustainability, Social Justice, and Religious Creativity* (Washington, DC: Georgetown University Press, 2013).

ecotheologies, earth stories, and ecomemories is an important step in ecowomanist method. Whether the earth stories engage arguments about the feminization of the earth, reveal parallel oppressions suffered by enslaved African women and the earth, or point to strategies of earth justice that emerge out of women's circles, a moral imperative for earth justice consistently arises. For this reason, earth justice serves as a primary value of ecowomanism. The process of studying, observing, and then gleaning values like this one from the wisdom of these women's epistemologies, agricultural knowledge, and ecomemories provides helpful resources from which to frame environmental justice responses to climate change.

Ecomemory refers to the collective and individual memory of the earth and relationship to and with the earth. It can be a collective set of values that guide the earth commitments of an entire community or a singular story that reflects themes or values about the environment and one's connection to the earth. In many cases, ecomemory is passed down through different generations and considered a part of family and communal legacy and intellectual heritage. George Washington Carver revolutionized the field of industrial biotechnology by using science to develop more than 300 industrial uses for peanuts, sweet potatoes, and other crops, making them more valuable and boosting farm profits. Carver's inventions, knowledge, and expertise of farming empowered thousands of black people and offer one example of ecomemory.[20] This kind of collective ecomemory not only serves to show an interest in the environment but provides a particular history of partnering with the earth. As feminist scholar and cultural critic bell hooks reminds us, it is precisely the agricultural knowledge that shapes so much of African American lineage in North America and throughout the diaspora. In her essay "Touching the Earth," hooks calls for a deep study and mining of the ecomemory of black peoples. Pointing to the empowering

---

[20] For more, see Christina Vella, *George Washington Carver: A Life* (Baton Rouge: Louisiana State University Press, 2015).

nature of the relationship between black peoples and the earth for the purpose of self-recovery from white supremacy and self-determination, hooks writes, "Living close to nature, black folks were able to cultivate a spirit of wonder and reverence for life. Growing food to sustain life and flowers to please the soul, they were able to make a connection with the earth that was ongoing and life-affirming. They were witnesses to beauty."[21] This act of witnessing, described in a religious sense, is in itself a spiritual experience that connects the being (self), the Spirit, and the earth. Drawing on the theme of interconnectedness articulated in the first chapter, and reflective of an African cosmology, the act of witnessing the earth's beauty that hooks describes is evidence of a relational connection between the earth, as *the beautiful* being honored, observed, and enjoyed (but not consumed) by the witness, *the being*. According to the ethical mandate of earth justice woven into many African tribes and established in the history of many African American churches (from the hush harbor movement to the present day), the relational condition between the *beautiful* (earth) and the *being* (human) is that both are honored in a kind of mutually enhancing relationship—one never exploiting or dominating the other.

This kind of relationship between the beautiful (earth) and the being as witness is also made evident by many Native American cosmologies and understandings about humans' relationship with the earth. In fact, hooks's writing notes the very close relationship historically between black and African peoples and Native Americans. She writes,

> From the moment of their first meeting, Native American and African people shared with one another a respect for the life giving forces of nature, of the earth. African settlers in Florida taught the Creek Nation runaways, the "Seminoles," methods for rice cultivation.

---

[21] bell hooks, *Sisters of the Yam: Black Women and Self-Recovery* (New York: South End Press, 2005), 137.

Native peoples taught recently arrived black folks all about the many uses of corn. . . . Sharing the reverence for the earth, black and red people helped one another remember that, despite the white man's ways, the land belonged to everyone.[22]

Similar to the recognition of interconnectedness in the earth community that was an intricate part of African American life and the awareness of the healing power of the earth to reconnect one to a sense of belonging, Native American peoples also recognized the power of earth to help one recognize the innate beauty and goodness of the self and all beings. Prophetically warning people of the dangers of dehumanization in white supremacist culture, and foreseeing the importance of such current movements as Black Lives Matter, Chief Luther Standing Bear recalls the ecowisdom of the Lakota: "The old Lakota was wise. He knew that man's heart away from nature becomes hard; he knew the lack of respect for growing, living things soon led to lack of respect of humans too."[23]

Recognition of the deep power of *being* recovery, a recovery of a knowing and sense of belonging and connection to all beings and the earth community, helps to heal the terrorizing impact of dehumanization normative in practices of white supremacy. This way of honoring experience and mining ecomemory is such an important first step in the ecowomanist method. Taking this step helps to fill in the gap of normative discourse about the environmental movement (traditionally not inclusive of African American history). African American environmental history and ecomemory specifically help to fill in the gap and provide sources for doing constructive ecowomanist

---

[22] Ibid., 137.

[23] Chief Luther Standing Bear, quoted in Llewellyn Vaughan-Lee, ed., *Spiritual Ecology: The Cry of the Earth* (Point Reyes, CA: Golden Sufi Center, 2013), 101.

thought and practice. Recovering ecomemory empowers African peoples to self-determine and act for earth justice.

Ecomemory as Countermemory

Ecomemory is actually countermemory. It is, as womanist scholar Emilie M. Townes explains, a "reconstitution" of normative history or metahistory that often discounts, denies, or rejects African American environmental history and the histories of peoples of color as a part of environmental history. Clarifying how the signifier "counter" is used in the concept, Townes explains that the "counter" in countermemory is not a rejection, but rather the

> reconstitution of history . . . the patient and persistent work of mining the motherlode of African American religious life. It is the methodological strategy that helps combat the hollow legacy of this kind of gross iconization of black identity. . . . It can provide hope in the midst of [environmental] degradation, and strength to continue to put one foot in front of the other in movements for justice. Countermemory has the potential to challenge the false generalizations and gross stereotypes often found in what passes for "history" in the United States. Countermemories can disrupt our status quo because they do not rest solely or wholly on objectivity or facts. They materialize from emotions and sights and sounds and touch and smell. They come from the deepest part of who we are. Countermemories are dynamic and spark new configurations of meaning.[24]

In ecowomanism, ecomemory is a form of countermemory that *reconstitutes* traditional environmental history that too

---

[24] Emilie M. Townes, *Womanist Ethics and the Cultural Production of Evil* (New York: Palgrave Macmillan, 2006), 45–46.

often overlooks, or ignores, the voices, experiences, and histories of black peoples. Instead, ecomemory begins from the central point of black and African life, and centers the perspectives, voices, and experience of African peoples. Moreover, ecowomanism's interdisciplinary approach expands normative environmental discourse by weaving in disciplines of art, literature, ethics, geography, and agriculture as these disciplines reflect African American environmental and religious history. The awareness of this ecomemory helps break through artificial claims that the environmental justice movement is just a *white people's* movement. Echoing the call by Walker for *all* people to become conscious of how structural oppression works and encourage all people and especially black peoples to get involved with the environmental justice movement, ecowomanism also claims, "As individuals we must join others. No time to quibble about survival being 'a white issue.' No time to claim you don't live here too."[25] As a first methodological step to ecowomanism, mining ecomemory simultaneously pushes back, critiquing traditional forms of environmental history that leave out the histories of peoples of color, and pushes forward social justice commitments to be incorporated within the environmental movement.[26]

---

[25] Alice Walker, "Nuclear Madness: What You Can Do," in *In Search of Our Mothers' Gardens: Womanist Prose* (New York: Harcourt Brace Jovanovich, 1983), 345.

[26] The relationship between ecomemory and an African sense of time linking past, present, and future is also an important aspect of study. While the subject of time goes beyond the focus of this chapter, it is important to note how ecomemory functions in the spirit of "*sankofa*." This adrikra symbol, from Ghanaian culture in West Africa, symbolizes the deep value of history or, in the case of ecomemory, as a source from which to draw wisdom on how to move forward into the future. In this sense, the concept of ecomemory is also mining earth stories from the past while simultaneously honoring earth stories and strategies of environmental justice in the present (such as responses to climate change) as well as earth stories of the future (i.e., how climate change will impact the

Mining Ecomemory—
The Work of Alice Walker as Ecowomanist Source

One example of how the first step of honoring experience or mining ecomemory is applied comes from the study, the work, and the writings of Walker. In her essay "The Only Reason You Want to Go to Heaven Is That You Have Been Driven Out of Your Mind . . . ," Walker documents an important ecomemory, a story reflective of themes and values about the environment and one's connection to the earth that has been passed down in the Walker family as a part of family legacy. The story told is actually a story from and about Walker's mother and her divine mystical experience of being revived by the earth's healing powers even in the midst of being confronted with and surviving multiple oppressions trying to sharecrop, educate her children, and raise a healthy youngster simultaneously. Walker writes,

> I remember my mother telling me of a time when she was hugely pregnant and had an enormous field of cotton, twenty-five or thirty acres, to chop, that is, to thin and weed. Her older children were in school, from which she refused to take them, her youngest trailed behind her and fell asleep in the furrows. My father, who was laborer, dairyman, and chauffeur, had driven the bosslady to town. As my mother looked out over the immense acreage still to be covered, she felt so ill she could barely lift the hoe. Never had she felt so alone. Coming to the end of a row, she lay down under a tree and asked to die. Instead, she fell into a deep sleep, and when she awakened, she was fully restored. In fact, she felt wonderful, as if a healing breeze had touched her soul. She picked up the hoe and continued her work.[27]

future). Again, additional study of the relationship between ecowomanism and time is encouraged.

[27] Alice Walker, "The Only Reason You Want to Go to Heaven Is That

Walker's reflection on the earth story of her mother is one example of how the first step of an ecowomanist method can be applied. Here she documents the experience of a woman of African descent, her mother, and describes how she faced insurmountable odds, combating structural oppression through the very act of toiling as a sharecropper on land the Walker family did not "own," how she did so even as she was "hugely" pregnant, and while simultaneously offering a parental "eye" over her younger child who had fallen asleep in the field. The structural oppression, reflective of the unfair system of sharecropping designed to keep black southerners enslaved to landowners and bound to the land so as to physically, emotionally, and mentally exhaust them, so they could not advance themselves by getting an education, as context, is as much a part of the story as her mother's level of exhaustion. In fact, one literary reading of the text is that her mother's exhaustion in the story reads as a woman tired of the structurally oppressive system of sharecropping that forced her and her family to work day in and day out in order to provide food and a livelihood for their family, even as their hard labor unfairly lined the pockets of an oppressive landowner.

Noting the loneliness her mother felt, stuck in the middle of an impossibly unjust and unfair situation, Walker writes pointedly about the "healing breeze" of the earth and how this restorative nature's breath not only restored her mother with physical strength, but with emotional fortitude and encouragement. "What God restored my mother?" Walker continues, posing a critically reflective question and thus inviting step two of an ecowomanist method: reflection on experience. "Was it the God who said women deserved to suffer and were evil anyway, or was it the God of nonjudgmental Nature calming and soothing her with the green coolness of the tree she slept under

---

You Have Been Driven Out of Your Mind (Off Your Land and Out of Your Lover's Arms): Clear Seeing Inherited Religion and Reclaiming the Pagan Self," in *Anything We Love Can Be Saved: A Writer's Activism* (New York: Random House, 1997), 13.

and the warm earth she lay upon?"[28] Walker's reflection on her mother's earth story and experience with nature is a stunning example of the first two steps of an ecowomanist method. The passage itself honors the experience of Mrs. Walker and documents her ecomemory.

In this section, the first step of an ecowomanist method, to honor experience or mining ecomemory, has been explicated. The concept of *ecomemory* and the related term *countermemory* have also been explained. While this section focused on the example of agricultural knowledge as an example of ecomemory, there are other examples of ecomemory worth mentioning. Agricultural memory is another example of ecomemory referring to the knowledge developed by enslaved Africans over generations of planting cotton, rice, tobacco, and other crops on southern plantations. In addition, knowledge of the environment shared by those enslaved Africans trying to escape to the North along the Underground Railroad is another example of ecomemory. More specifically, the hope and actual guiding light of the North Star are referenced in many slave narratives and serve as primary examples of embodied ecomemory (hope). Hope as ecomemory carries an active, spiritual, and physical significance for African Americans.[29] This can be seen through additional critical reflection on the agency-producing power of ecomemory. We see this illustrated, and perhaps experience it ourselves, in the *telling* of the earth story (testimony) by Mrs. Walker to her daughter, Alice.

Since Mrs. Walker is reflecting on the spiritual experience of being revived by sacred earth, sharing it makes this telling of ecomemory an earth-honoring faith story or testimony. Illustrating the practice of *testimony* from the African American church tradition, Mrs. Walker's sharing of ecomemory transforms into an agency-producing proof narrative about

---

[28] Ibid.

[29] While it goes beyond the scope of this chapter, additional theological construction of hope, as an embodied form of ecomemory, is an important aspect of ecowomanism.

the power of the sacred or divine healing power of the earth. While it is the case that Mrs. Walker was herself a Christian woman, and likely would have interpreted the healing narrative as a testament of God's healing power through earth, it is significant that Alice Walker's interpretation of her mother's testimony leads to a kind of earth testimony of her own, pointing to the divine as earth. Given that Alice Walker's ecospirituality has a very different point of origin than the Christian roots of her mother, it is important to note that Walker's own ecomemory of her mother's story may in fact lead to a different understanding of the sacredness of earth than her mother. That is, as Walker explains, there is a very different creation narrative and dogma that Mrs. Walker may have used to frame her testimony of the "healing breeze" she experienced as a woman informed by the traditional form of Christianity practiced in that time and place.[30] Alice Walker's own interpretation of her mother's ecomemory seems to spring from a different root, so to speak. That is, regardless of the Christian frame that Mrs. Walker may have applied to her understanding of the healing experience of earth, the freedom enmeshed in ecomemory invites her daughter, Alice Walker, to interpret the ecomemory differently and come up with another ecomemory—inspired by the premise that it was the earth itself that healed her mother. Her interpretation of her mother's ecomemory does not necessitate a Christian God, or that she accept the premise or frame of a Christian interpretation of creation, to be empowered by her mother's ecomemory. In short, ecomemory gives root to ecomemory—across religious and spiritual traditions. This, as we will see in Chapter Four, is a liberating and important aspect of ecomemory and its function within ecowomanism in that it can serve as a conceptual base (and methodological step) for interreligious dialogue about climate change and environmental justice.

Mrs. Walker's ecomemory is agency producing. It not only serves as a spiritual, and perhaps theological, base from which

---

[30] Walker, "The Only Reason You Want to Go to Heaven . . . ," 3–27.

to create multiple ecomemories (sometimes reflecting different ecological and spiritual perspectives), but the very telling or sharing of Mrs. Walker's ecomemory is empowering. It gives voice to a black woman's story, an earth story about her relationship with and to the earth. One can imagine Mrs. Walker sharing this story with her daughter, Alice Walker, as an empowering, agency-producing, and life-giving part of the process of sharing ecomemory itself. Sharing ecomemory is itself an empowering act and an act of earth justice.

The first methodological step of ecowomanism therefore is dynamic in its purpose and function. The honoring of experience, or mining ecomemory, not only documents the history of African American environmental history, it simultaneously uncovers ecowisdom and ecowomanist values such as those reflective of Mrs. Walker's experience of the sacred healing power of the earth. At the same time, the act of sharing ecomemory is itself agency producing and an empowering act of justice. The explanation of both of these aspects of ecomemory shows the significance of honoring the environmental experience or ecomemory of women of African descent. This study can open the door for new epistemologies for the study, theory, and practice of environmental justice, as well as empower actual acts of justice.[31] As witnessed from the story and in Walker's reflection on her mother's experience, several themes emerge that correspond with an ecowomanist earth-honoring faith and value system. Reflection on these themes for the purpose of mining meaning, values,

---

[31] Ecomemory is filled with images of beauty but also consist of images of terror. This paradox known as the *"beauty-to-burden"* paradox, explicated by Kimberly N. Ruffin, highlights a dynamism that functions within the concept of ecomemory. Kimberly N. Ruffin, *Black on Earth: African American Ecoliterary Traditions* (Athens: University of Georgia Press, 2010). This concept informs ecowomanist responses. I would argue that this also informs black environmental liberation theology. For more on black environmental liberation theology, see Glave, "Black Environmental Liberation Theology," 189–99.

and possible strategies of earth justice begins the process of step two of the ecowomanist method: critical reflection on experience.

Step Two:
Critical Reflection on Experience and Ecomemory

Critical reflection on African and African American environmental experience and ecomemory is the second step of the ecowomanist method. This type of reflection takes place in a number of different ways, but for purposes of this chapter, we will explore shared ecomemory that might dispel myths and speak truths about systemic oppressions and structural evil. This line of questioning illustrates a mode of reflection that is critical and even deconstructive in nature. Then we will turn toward reflection that is constructive in nature that helps us to mine values and resources in African American religious traditions, liberation spiritualities, and ecotheologies. Examining these sources and the strategies that emerge from them helps interrupt a logic of domination used to establish a theoretical frame that perpetuates environmental degradation. By connecting the results of the critical analysis (deconstructive) with the sources of ecowomanist strategy and theory (constructive), this second step of reflection helps identify ecowomanist themes. These themes—including the parallel oppressions suffered by women of color and specifically women of African descent and the earth, the history of colonization of African peoples and ecological colonialism, and the power in the signification of the word *bound* and the phrase *bound to earth* used by ecowomanist scholars to reclaim connection with the earth—provide specific starting points for additional analysis in step three of the method. Two of those themes will be discussed here; a third theme referring to the history of colonization of African peoples and ecological colonialism will be discussed in the fourth step.

In order to more clearly identify these themes, we return to the critical reflection of ecomemory detailed in Walker's essay.[32] One way the second step of an ecowomanist method can be applied is by examining the shared experience of structural oppression that Mrs. Walker and the earth both experience in the story. The system of sharecropping was designed as an extension of slavery of African peoples. Diffusing the power of the law and the Emancipation Proclamation, which declared all enslaved black and African peoples free, the system of sharecropping was designed to trap the formerly enslaved into an oppressive economic system of never-ending toil and disadvantage. Landowners, traditionally former slave owners (and sometimes wealthy blacks who gained land after the Civil War), contracted formerly enslaved families to work the land for a fee. Since most newly freed people had no capital or resources to pay for use of the land, they were connived into giving away their labor for free and forced to pay off their debts with the promise of future crops. If the crops failed for any reason, the lives and lifestyles of the sharecroppers were threatened if not ruined completely. This constant reality of debt, combined with the constant threat of terror that could be unleashed on their families at any moment, kept most sharecroppers docile and silent regarding any form of resistance that might expose the unfair capitalist exploitation system of the landowner.

The system of sharecropping or tenant farming rarely resulted in farmers making enough money to purchase land or make a profit from their labor. Just when it appeared that a family was in a good position to acquire enough money to purchase land or make a sizable profit, the landowner would surprisingly increase the price for tools necessary to work the land, seed for planting, or the *tenant's rent* as the cost to work the land itself. The never-ending, death-dealing, almost pointless daily toil eroded the souls and stole the hope of

---

[32] Walker, "The Only Reason You Want to Go to Heaven . . . ," 3–27.

many farmers and their families. In many African American communities, only the chance to gain an education in order to advance the opportunity for social uplift for the family and a hope in God inspired them to survive this living state of terror. The empowerment offered by black faith insisted that God was on the side of the oppressed,[33] and heard the sorrowful cries of those breaking under the unfair economic and white supremacist system. Community became a central value for sharecropping families, since it was the support from others in the community that provided motivation and enough hope to go on. Thus, from a constructionist ecowomanist frame, community can be gleaned as a primary ecowomanist value.

When we reflect on the ecomemory of Mrs. Walker with this kind of understanding of the context, new revelations about the ecowisdom from the story become clear. As a woman of African descent contending with these historical realities of racism, classism, sexism, and poverty as a sharecropping mother in the South, we can imagine Mrs. Walker grappling with and being overwhelmed with the complex dynamism of the brutal system. Like many sharecroppers, the system forced a kind of enslaving relationship to the land upon her, and yet her ecomemory clearly tells of a kind of empowering relationship she had with the earth. That is, even as she receives restoration from the "healing breeze" of the earth in the story, the reader can sense her overwhelming exhaustion at having toiled in the field.

The paradoxical relationship that Mrs. Walker has with the earth in the story, as one *bound to* the earth, as one forced to work the land, and as one *bound or connected to* the earth in divine relationship with the sacred earth, is important to acknowledge from an ecowomanist perspective. The double entendre of my use of the word *bound* should not be lost on

---

[33] James H. Cone, *God of the Oppressed* (Maryknoll, NY: Orbis Books, 1997).

the reader. As a way of pointing to the paradoxical relationship that Mrs. Walker and many women of African descent have with the earth, the double meaning of *bound* illustrates the complex way African Americans understand their relationship or connection with the land. Kimberly N. Ruffin conceptualizes this kind of paradoxical relationship that black women and African American peoples have historically had with the earth as the *beauty-to-burden* paradox. She explains how African Americans' environmental experiences are unique because the movement of the beauty of nature found in black peoples' deep awareness and connection with the calming rhythms of the earth is simultaneously marked by the horrors of the lynching of black bodies, the realities of rape and oppression of black enslaved women and men, the domination and cruelty of white racism, and the control and abusive ways of white male slave owners and white women mistresses. According to Ruffin, this, too, colors the reality of African American environmental history: ecomemory. The legacy of white supremacy woven through the law of racial discrimination during the Jim and Jane Crow era and the *problem of the color line* as Du Bois explained it are all aspects of African American environmental history. The beauty-to-burden paradox illustrates how African peoples' experiences of earth connection (beauty) cannot be set apart as the sole theoretical base for shaping environmental thought or policy. It shows that African American ecomemories are also infused with individual and collective memories of racial hatred and brutality. Ruffin explains the ecological paradox further, saying it

pinpoints the dynamic influence of the natural and social order on African American experience and outlook. For instance, an ecological burden is placed on those who are racialized negatively, and they therefore suffer economically and environmentally because of their degraded status. Simultaneously, however, the experience of ecological beauty results from individual and collective attitudes toward nature that undercut the experience of racism and its related evils.[34]

Ruffin's articulation of the beauty-to-burden paradox helps deepen the kind of critical reflection necessary for the second step of an ecowomanist method and provides a base for conducting additional analysis in step three of the method: applying womanist intersectional analysis.

Step Three:
Womanist Intersectional Analysis

Before moving forward to explicate step three, it is helpful to review how the first two steps of the method have been illustrated in the book thus far. Chapter One of this book illustrates the first step of an ecowomanist method by honoring experience. This chapter shared the experience of my own eco-autobiography and established a historical, cultural, and religious framing of my own ecomemory. One significant aspect of my experience and most ecomemory is that it relates and connects to the stories of so many African peoples' (and some non-African peoples') experiences with the earth. It is significant that my experience as an African American whose lineage was deeply informed by the Great Migration can be linked to the experience of six million other African Americans' stories, shaping a collective ecomemory. That is, the ecomemory of my own heritage illustrates themes of loss of community and displacement from lands as well as stories of hope. Even though they were fleeing the threat of illegal lynching and experiences of racial hatred in the South, my grandparents, along with many black farmers, regained a sense of agency, self-determination, and earth community by building up and establishing the black farming community. As short as the life span of this community may have been, the agency and drive toward a

---

[34] Ruffin, *Black on Earth*, 3.

liberating relationship with the land that these farmers embodied are worthy values of study for ecowomanism.

Additional reflection on my ecomemory, using a constructive frame, reveals ecowisdom gleaned from the earth story of my grandparents. I value the agricultural genius that my grandparents embodied (reflective of the African virtue of improvisation),[35] which enabled them to be able to plant roots in the rocky soil of Colorado and produce a harvest in spite of having only known the fertile soil of Mississippi all their lives.

Drawing connections and critically reflecting on the collective ecomemories of African peoples is a part of the work of step two of an ecowomanist method: critical reflection on experience. In the previous section, an ecomemory as told by Alice Walker serves as a point of analysis for developing the critical reflection. Here reflection on the story of Mrs. Walker helps clarify the beauty-to-burden paradox of African American environmental experience and bring a focus on themes including:

1. parallel oppressions shared by women of African descent and the earth; and
2. a critique of the colonization of peoples of color and colonial ecology, and the agency-producing side aspect of ecomemory and ecowomanism itself, which can be seen in part by the move to reclaim the African American heritage of environmental history that can be healing and provides maps for self-recovery in African American communities today.

Step three invites an even deeper move into analysis of ecomemory and applies womanist analysis for the purpose of identifying ecowomanist themes and values. It uses race, class, gender, and intersectional analysis to highlight strategies

---

[35] Peter J. Paris, *The Spirituality of African Peoples: The Search for a Common Moral Discourse* (Minneapolis: Fortress Press, 1995).

of earth justice that women of African descent have culti-
vated over the years in response to cases of environmental
racism and climate injustice.

Race–class–gender analysis can most easily be applied by
inviting critique and posing questions about structural violence
based on race, racism, or racial privilege; class and economic
privilege; and gender, sexism, and gender privilege. Womanist
intersectional analysis, however, is also inclusive of analysis
emerging around sexual justice, critiquing heterosexist norms,
and ageism, and is critical of any form of systematic oppression that creates disparities between one sociocultural group
and another. For example, when access to basic rights, such as
health, education, and a safe environment (water, soil, etc.), are
denied because of some form of discrimination against people,
based on their race, class, gender, sexual orientation, age, religion, nationality, or regional influence, then such womanist
intersectional analysis is important. It raises questions that
interrupt the patterns of structural oppression and attempt
to change immoral and unethical behavior and action that is
complicit in a system of structural oppression.

Womanist intersectional analysis uses a multidimensional
lens designed to uncover how racial, economic, gender, sexual, and environmental injustice may constrict the building of
moral communities living with and in the earth. The analysis
applies critical deconstructive approaches in order to detail
the stories, circumstances, and moral ideas about earth justice
articulated by women of African descent. It is also constructive in that it proposes sets of values and systems of ethics
that honor the humanity of all people, and fights for the full
liberation and justice of African American women, children,
and men as members of the global human community living
in the fullness of the earth community.[36]

From inside the third step of ecowomanist method, let
us now enlarge our perspective, taking a wider view of the

---

[36] Additional information on the tasks of womanist ethics can be
seen in Riggs, *Awake, Arise and Act.*

method. The ecowomanist method is a spiral, and, as such, the methodological steps are interchangeable. One example of this is how step one, honoring experience, and step three, engaging womanist intersectional analysis, both reflect the critical deconstructive and constructive approaches to ecowomanism. Attending to the deconstruction of myths, steps one and three both follow a deconstructive angle to highlight previously silenced or overlooked experiences and perspectives of black women and people of color in the shaping of environmental ethics, environmental justice, and environmentalists' discourse. That is, the environmental concerns and perspectives of women of color, specifically African and African American women, are not considered normative, and thus are not incorporated into the environmental movement's conceptual frames. Highlighting elements of racial bias and practices of social exclusion normative in traditional environmental groups, sociologist Dorceta E. Taylor points out that the development of the environmental movement did not include or consider the experiences of people of color until more recently. Therefore, the structure, conceptual frames, and cultural norms and assumptions made by the white middle- to upper-class (often) male founders of most traditional environmental groups did not consider the voices, perspectives, and theoretical framing of women of African descent and communities of color valid epistemologies. Taylor describes the disconnect best in her essay "The Rise of the Environmental Justice Paradigm: Injustice Framing and the Social Construction of Environmental Discourses"[37] as she describes the different social locations from which environmental activists come and influence:

> Mainstream environmental activists and environmental justice activists are, for the most part, in different social locations. As such, they have vastly different environmental experiences, and those experiences influence how they perceive environmental issues, construct

---

[37] Taylor, "Environmental Justice Paradigm."

discourses, organize campaigns, and develop activist strategies. In addition, their social locations endow them with access to different kinds and amounts of resources; the availability of resources influences the strategies used and the kind of movements that activists build. Consequently, mainstream environmentalists who might count lawmakers among their personal, political, or professional networks are more likely to use lobbying as an activist strategy, whereas environmental justice activists, with much less access to Congress and other powerful political bodies in the country, are more likely to use direct-action strategies such as protests and rallies as part of their campaigns. As further discussions show, social location and people's experiences and perceptions of the issues will also influence the type of movement they develop.[38]

Paramount to Taylor's essay is her description of the environmental justice paradigm as "the first paradigm to link environment and race, class, gender and social justice concerns in an explicit framework."[39] Rather than using normative paradigms or pathways of environmental activism, such as the *dominant social*, *exploitive capitalist*, *romantic environmental*, or *new environmental* paradigms that have historically shaped preservationist, conservationist, or romanticized nature ideals, the environmental justice paradigm offers a different entry point. It problematizes the conceptual base of these paradigms, based on their reliance on normative assumptions of white privilege, and exposes how the history of white supremacy is woven into the conceptual frame of ecological colonialism. Rather than ignoring the impact race, class, and gender bias has on environmental health disparities globally, the environmental justice paradigm links social-justice issues to environmental justice. It recognizes that peoples of color have a very

---

[38] Ibid., 510.
[39] Ibid., 542.

different entry point into environmental ethical discourse and argues that their experience as earth (i.e., enslaved Africans were considered land and property) necessitates a completely different paradigm concerning earth and earth justice. Again, Taylor is helpful here. The quotation is worthy of including at length.

The environmental experiences of people of color differ markedly from that of Whites; therefore, it is not surprising that their environmental activism, agendas, and paradigms differ from those constructed by middle- and working-class Whites. This is the case because, first, the history of the environmental activism of people of color is one of trying to redefine how they relate to the environment (in terms of their living and working conditions and recreational opportunities). That redefinition has three components: autonomy or self-determination, land rights, and civil or human rights. Throughout history, Whites have accumulated and controlled resources by appropriating land and labor and by controlling the movement of people of color. In addition, the period of conquest was characterized by destruction of indigenous cultural systems. Whites, however, were free to express themselves and develop the kinds of relations with the land as they saw fit. Although some exploited the land, others sought alternative ways of relating to the land.

The latter developed paradigms to reflect their beliefs. People of color did not have these choices. Since the 17th century, people of color have been enslaved, pushed onto reservations, forcibly removed from their territories, interned, or made to toil under harsh conditions (with limited opportunities for upward mobility). In fact, if land was not appropriated from people of color through treaties, warfare, or "purchase," there were a variety of legal and crooked means through which they lost land or were prevented from acquiring it. In addition, people of color had little or no choice about where they lived, what jobs they did, or how they interacted with the land. . . . Consequently, one of the enduring struggles of people of color is that of self-determination—the struggle to define who they are and how they interact with the land. It is also a quest to discover how much of their traditional skills and cultural practices can be recaptured and reinstated. Efforts to attain autonomy are closely aligned to the struggle for land and upholding treaty rights (i.e., the struggle to reclaim appropriated territories, fishing and water rights, etc.).

The third prong of their activism revolves around the struggle for civil and human rights—the desire to be treated fairly and with human dignity. It is not surprising, therefore, that the environmental discourses of people of color are framed around concepts like autonomy, self-determination, access to resources, fairness and justice, and civil and human rights. These concepts are not found in mainstream environmental discourses. This is the case because the mainstream environmental discourse was developed primarily by free, White males who were either wealthy or had access to wealthy people. These men, free to develop capitalist enterprises, roamed the outdoors at will, recreated when or where they pleased, and constructed environmental discourses that reflected their cultural backgrounds, lifestyles, experiences, and thinking. From their vantage point (social location), issues of autonomy and freedom had little or no resonance or salience. These were not issues that concerned them enough to warrant including them in the environmental discourses they were developing. They did not see how such issues were connected to environmental activism. Indeed, freedom and autonomy were privileges they had and took for granted. Thus, they developed discourses around resource depletion, degradation, and resource management.[40]

---

[40] Ibid., 542.

The three components of the environmental justice paradigm —autonomy or self-determination, land rights, and civil or human rights—that Taylor describes can also serve as ecowomanist values, and can be gleaned from each of the methodological steps. Steps one and two of the method provide resources for establishing autonomy. The same is true of step four, critically examining African and African American history and tradition for models of autonomy and self-determination (e.g., the establishment of Dearfield, Colorado, a black farming community). Step three of the ecowomanist method is also reflective of the three components of an environmental justice paradigm in that it signals the importance of exposing systems of injustice and the negative impact they can have on the rights of people of color. This includes people of color's environmental rights. Applying womanist intersectional analysis (and all of the steps) is therefore congruent with Taylor's environmental justice paradigm. As such, ecowomanism adopts an environmental justice paradigm. In the history of African American environmental justice movements, there is a deep history of activism that uncovers unique theories and helps us explore the synthesis between ecology and faith commitments, earth care and faith, and *green theologies* that provide a foundation for earth-honoring faiths. Finding out more about these forms of activism is made possible by moving to the fourth step of the ecowomanist method: critically examining African and African American history and tradition.

Step Four:
Critically Examining African and
African American History and Tradition

The application of womanist intersectional analysis prompts us to think about the paradox within African American and African diasporic environmental history more deeply. For this, we engage a fourth step: critically examining African and African American history and tradition. One way that this examination takes place is by building on the themes that have been gleaned by previous analysis, namely, the themes of (1) parallel oppressions suffered by women of color, and specifically women of African descent, and the earth; (2) history of the colonialization of African peoples and ecological colonialism; and (3) power in the signification of the word *bound* and the phrase *bound to earth* used by ecowomanist scholars. The first and third themes have already been examined in the explication of step three. For the purpose of this fourth methodological step, it is helpful to examine African and African American history and tradition by interrogating the parallels between the history of colonization of African peoples and ecological colonialism.

The latter term, *ecological colonialism*, is described best by African theologian Edward Antonio, writing about the parallel ways in which the Western practice of colonization has also infected environmentalist paradigms.[41] He writes of the sixteenth-century mode of Western thought to colonialize African peoples and to invade, steal, consume, and dominate the cultures of African peoples. This mode parallels the consuming attitudes of traditional environmentalist claims that a return to Africa will uncover a fresh interpretative lens, leading to healthy responses to climate change, a result of the same infected practice of colonialism, interwoven with a deep commitment to global capitalism. Colonialism, a system of exploitation and abuse of cultures, properties, peoples, and lands for the sake of greed and empire-building of European culture and commerce, is complicit in enslaving millions of African peoples across the planet. According to Antonio, the impetus undergirding colonialism is the same seed that gives birth to the idea of colonial ecology. Arguing, like actor and activist Jesse

---

[41] Edward P. Antonio, "Ecology as Experience in African Indigenous Religions," in *Living Stones in the Household of God: The Legacy and Future of Black Theology*, ed. Linda E. Thomas, 146–57 (Minneapolis: Fortress Press, 2003).

Williams, that African peoples' cultures and lands have for too long been commodified by Europeans and white culture, while black and African peoples are left exploited and assaulted,[42] Antonio states that traditional environmentalists have conceptualized paradigms that consistently reify images of black and African bodies as *nobodies* (except for the ways they can create value for whiteness). This move implicitly reestablishes European rule over the continental sacred lands of Africa.

Reflecting on the stereotypical premise made by a fellow environmentalist that African peoples are *closer to nature*, Antonio strikes at the claim that essentially states that, in the midst of the crisis state of climate change, (white) environmentalists have only to turn to the ancient past of African people to redeem and restore themselves. Antonio points to the colonializing aspects of such an assumption, writing that even the environmentalist ways of thinking are poisoned by a colonial mind-set.

> [T]he alleged kinship of Africans to nature emerges from this as a socially constructed and politically contested idea in which contradictory romantic notions about the environment are at work. The basis of this was of course that will to power that has dominated so much of Western thought since the sixteenth century. The colonial context provided an ideal setting for the

---

[42] Jesse Williams, BET Humanitarian Award 2016 Speech, http://genius.com/9835857. "Peace, peace . . . We've [African Americans] been floating this country on credit for centuries, yo, and we're done watching and waiting while this invention called whiteness uses and abuses us, burying black people out of sight and out of mind while extracting our culture, our dollars, our entertainment like oil—black gold, ghettoizing and demeaning our creations then stealing them, gentrifying our genius and then trying us on like costumes before discarding our bodies like rinds of strange fruit. The thing is though . . . the thing is that just because we're magic doesn't mean we're not real."

exercise of this will to power both on other cultures and on nature. . . . The idea that indigenous peoples are close to nature is not politically innocent. It is linked to various romantic notions of nature in European thought, of translating the very different worldviews within which traditional ecologies developed and functioned into ways of thinking and modes of practice that would make them relevant or applicable to the global culture of late capitalism. Although the appeal to the language of kinship is meant to hint at the possibility of just such a translation, it is in fact the need for kinship that points to the lack of fit or congruence between traditional and modern experiences of ecological disaster.[43]

The parallel between the colonization of the earth and the colonization of black and African bodies throughout the history of the transatlantic slave trade up to the present is an important theme in ecowomanist thought. Not only is this reflective of the need to examine the truth of African and African American history and tradition, but also a call to examine the myths that have been constructed about this history. In fact, one of the reasons returning to a critical examination of African and African American environmental history is so important is that too often the myths and social constructions of African and African American history and tradition are so maligned that a constant reexamination is necessary. This constant reexamination is reflective of a larger womanist move to examine and critically self-examine one's interpretative lens and viewpoint.

In her edited volume *Deeper Shades of Purple: Womanism in Religion and Society*, author Stacey Floyd-Thomas discusses the significance of a reflective step as a womanist principle.[44]

---

[43] Antonio, "Ecology as Experience in African Indigenous Religions," 156–57.

[44] Stacey M. Floyd-Thomas, ed., *Deeper Shades of Purple: Womanism in Religion and Society* (New York: New York University Press, 2006).

Borrowing from the frame of Walker's definition of womanist, Floyd-Thomas suggests that a methodological move reflected within womanist analysis includes critical engagement of the field. Building on my essay contribution in that volume, "Womanist Humanism,"[45] I would argue that Floyd-Thomas's observation is on the right track, but that the critical examination must be pushed much further into the womanist scholar taking a critical self-examination of her own sources, socioeconomic background, and context (institutional, regional, religious, etc.). As I argue in *Gifts of Virtue, Alice Walker, and Womanist Ethics,* too often womanist scholars attempt to hide under the guise of faithful academics, all the while applying homophobic, elitist, and even malinformed categories based on a colorist, class, hierarchal, and racial bias. Womanism is not a competition, I argue; womanism is a way of being in community with all others in the earth community.[46]

Merging theory with praxis, ecowomanist method is deconstructive but also constructive in that the examination of African and African American religion and tradition opens to a fifth step that reveals historical and present-day examples of African and African American women who have found the courage to resist climate injustice. Whether laying their bodies down or singing spiritual songs in protest of large corporations responsible for leaking pollutants into the air, water, and soil, African American women have found courage and direction to fight for earth justice from their belief and faith. Engaging a kind of spiritual activism, these women have bolstered their agency and risen up in protest against environmental racism. A look at this kind of spiritual activism sets up the fifth step in an ecowomanist method: engaging transformation.

---

[45] Melanie L. Harris, "Womanist Humanism," in Floyd-Thomas, *Deeper Shades of Purple,* 211–25.

[46] Harris, *Gifts of Virtue, Alice Walker, and Womanist Ethics.*

Step Five:
Engaging Transformation

By examining the work of ecowomanist thinkers, writers, and activists, step five of the method explores the spiritual activism of selected ecowomanists, namely, Alice Walker, Valdina Oliveria Pinto, Rose Mary Amenga-Etego and Mercy Oduyoye. Specifically this method answers the following questions, and examines how black women practice their ecospirituality or earth-honoring faiths, which simultaneously influence their spiritual activism: What is unique about the earth-honoring faiths and ecospiritualities practiced by women of African descent that invites them to speak truth to power, and act and write boldly for earth justice? What are the unique resources embedded within African and African American religious tradition and spirituality that empower and lift up models of spiritual activism for environmental justice?

Building on womanist social analysis, which insists that structural evil be exposed, ecowomanist method engages a fifth step of *engaging transformation*. This step introduces *ecowomanist spirituality* as it is theorized and practiced by Walker, Amenga-Etego, Pinto, and Oduyoye. The latter two are discussed in more detail in Chapter Four.

The ecospirituality of Alice Walker has been discussed in my earlier work, most noteworthy in an essay entitled "Alice Walker and the Emergence of Ecowomanist Spirituality."[47] In this essay I argue that Walker's fiction and nonfiction writings provide a unique resource for ecowomanism and even map out theoretical and practical steps toward engaging ecowomanist praxis. Her essay "Only Justice Can Stop a Curse" is

---

[47] Melanie L. Harris, "Alice Walker and the Emergence of Ecowomanist Spirituality," in *Spirit and Nature: The Study of Christian Spirituality in a Time of Ecological Urgency*, ed. Timothy Hessell-Robinson and Ray Maria McNamara, 220–23 (Eugene, OR: Pickwick, Princeton Theological Monograph Series, 2011).

particularly instructive in that it prompts people of color, in particular, to get involved in an antinuclear and environmental movement, and reclaim earth as their home, too: "Earth is my home—though for centuries white people have tried to convince me I have no right to exist, except in the dirtiest, darkest corners of the globe."[48] Weaving analytical points that connect the realities of black women of African descent having to face white supremacy along with the struggle of the earth, Walker's essay here brilliantly shows how an ecowomanist way of being is rooted in commitments of social justice and human rights, as well as *earthling* rights to belong to the earth community.

The ecowomanist work and writings of Brazilian healer and Candomblé priestess and scholar Valdina Oliveria Pinto are most notably recorded in an essay entitled "Afro-Brazilian Religion, Resistance, and Environment: A Perspective from Candomblé."[49] In the interview translated by African American religion and ethnic studies scholar Dr. Rachel E. Harding, Pinto explains the transformative power of healing self, community, and earth reflected in Candomblé. Explaining the significance of the environment for the practice of the religion itself, she responds,

> There is no Candomblé, there is no cultivation of orixas, nkisis, voduns, or encantados (Amerindian indigenous spirits) without the natural world. . . . Nature communicates their essence. The essence of the orixas, nkisis, voduns is the plants; the essence is the land; the essence is water; the essence is a stone. The essence is the animals—even if it's just the little bitty animal that is so

---

[48] Alice Walker, "Only Justice Can Stop a Curse," in *In Search of Our Mothers' Gardens: Womanist Prose*, 338–42.

[49] Valdina Oliveria Pinto, "Afro-Brazilian Religion, Resistance, and Environment: A Perspective from Candomblé," *Worldviews: Global Religions, Culture, and Ecology* 20, no. 1, trans. Rachel E. Harding (2016): 76–86.

small we don't see, it's still present in the world. Nature speaks to us. Inside the phenomena of nature, that's where the orixa, the vodun, and the nkisi are.[50]

Reflective of an African indigenous cosmology that embraces interdependence with nature and a reverence of earth, Pinto's description models another perspective of ecowomanist spirituality. From an ecowomanist ethical perspective, it is also worth noting how the theme of resistance in the Afro-Brazilian peoples' struggle for civil rights is woven into the practice of Candomblé. Rather than embodying a binary construct within the tradition that separates the environmental from the sacred, Candomblé views the earth as sacred. This principle is not only in keeping with ecowomanist spirituality, but also reflective of the first and primary principle named by the Peoples of Color Summit on Environmental Justice in 1991. While written almost three decades ago, the principles themselves are still relevant for ecowomanist, social justice, and environmental ethics discourse today.[51]

Ecowomanist discourse is intentional in its inclusion of religious and ecowomanist spiritual perspectives across the diaspora. As such, the work of African feminist theologian Mercy Oduyoye is also significant in the work of ecowomanism. Some of her ecowomanist commitments can be witnessed in her essay "Earth Hope: A Letter."[52] The kind of intimate relationship that Oduyoye experiences with earth is one aspect of an ecowomanist relationality with the environment that sparks as a theme for ecowomanist dialogue and reflection. What is also important to note is the fluid spirituality that exists between Oduyoye's Christian orientation and cultural veneration of the earth as sacred. Partnering with God to transform climate justice into a reality is an element of her work that is witnessed by her ecowomanist practice and scholarship.

---

[50] Ibid., 80–81.

[51] Taylor, "The Rise of the Environmental Justice Paradigm," 566.

[52] In *Worldviews: Global Religions, Culture, and Ecology* 20, no. 1 (2016): 87–92.

The multiplicity of religious traditions and spiritualities engaged by ecowomanist thinkers, writers, scholars, and practitioners is a vibrant part of ecowomanist study and scholarship. Deepening the religious pluralism reflected in the study of the African diaspora, ecowomanism also reflects the varied religious, fluid spiritual, and dynamic perspectives of women of African descent. For this reason, and to enhance ecowomanist dialogue toward the goal of creating sustainable conversation about environmental justice from the perspective of a multiplicity of women of African descent, step six of the ecowomanist method acknowledges religious pluralism alive in African religious life and tradition, and invites dialogue about earth justice engaging these multiple perspectives.

Step Six:
Sharing Dialogue

Step six of the method, sharing interfaith and interreligious dialogue among ecowomanist earth-honoring faiths, also honors the ecospirituality of women of African descent. The earth is a concern to all religions. Whether embedded within the origin stories and religious narratives about how the planet was shaped, or emerging from particular principles about earth justice based on covenantal rules to honor God or be proper stewards of God's creation, most religious traditions embody an earth ethic that can guide an individual's faith and earth orientation. Because ecowomanism uplifts the ecological perspectives of women of African descent, and many of their religiosities reflect an African cosmology in which all things are understood to be interdependent, attention to the varieties of religious practice and identity among African women is also an important focus of ecowomanism.

Building from the arch of a third-wave womanist hallmark, interreligious dialogue for womanist religious thought incorporates attention to globalization, postcolonial theory, interdisciplinary approaches, and interreligious dialogue. Focusing on this aspect of ecowomanism expands the sources of ecowomanist reflection and analysis, helping to establish the development of new methods of analysis that connect theory with praxis and break new ground in interreligious dialogue about earth justice. In addition to responding to the need for interreligious methods that will speak to the urgency of climate change, this methodological step validates the various religious traditions incorporated in ecowomanism.

Step Seven:
Take Action for Earth Justice:
Teaching Ecowomanism

Step seven of the method is to take action for earth justice by making the link between social justice and earth justice. This involves building mutual approaches to share in the work of exposing what Townes calls the production of evil, protesting the logic of domination and abuse in all of its forms, naming and resisting structural and individual forms of violence, and replacing them with *truth force* and love. In addition to outlining how one can engage ecowomanist texts and resources, this step instructs the reader on ecowomanist pedagogy. As such, it outlines some of the basic themes of ecowomanism and how to present this in a college, university, or community classroom. Many of the pedagogical strategies introduced in Chapter Six come from teaching approaches that I have used in college and community classrooms, including classes taught as a part of the Earth-Honoring Faith seminar, a ten-year commitment of environmental justice teaching and praxis that I codirected, sponsored by the Ghost Ranch Educational Center.

Conclusion

While the process is steeped in the long history of womanist reflections about earth relatedness and spirituality, the overt naming of earth justice as a primary component of womanist concern and analysis is something new. As we examine the stories of women of African descent and hear about their own relationships with the earth, womanist analysis now shifts to include earth justice as a primary sphere of inquiry and examination. In a day and time when human and social transformation is so deeply interwoven with the future of the planet, earth justice is as important a justice concern for African peoples as all other justice concerns.

CHAPTER THREE

Critical Exploration of African and African American History and Tradition

In this chapter, the fourth methodological step of an ecowomanist method is engaged: critical exploration of African and African American history and tradition.[1] As such, in this chapter the work and ideas of African, African American, and black theologians, ethicists, environmental geographers, sociologists, literary artists, activists, and scholars are referenced as leaders shaping the discourse. One will note from this list that ecowomanist and environmental justice discourse is diverse, dialogical, interdisciplinary, and even interreligious. This important theoretical framing builds on three important hallmarks of third-wave womanism that I articulated in *Gifts of Virtue, Alice Walker, and Womanist Ethics*.[2] These hallmarks include

---

[1] This chapter is a revision of my previously published chapter "African American Environmental Religious Ethics and Ecowomanism," in *Routledge Handbook of Religion and Ecology* (New York: Routledge, 2017), 196–20, and is reprinted with permission.

[2] Melanie L. Harris, *Gifts of Virtue, Alice Walker, and Womanist Ethics* (New York: Palgrave Macmillan, 2010).

(1) the global links across the African diaspora and its peoples that recognize connections between worldviews, ethics, and cultures, as well as the parallels and common struggles experienced by African peoples as a result of globalization and the impact of climate change; (2) the necessity for interdisciplinary approaches to help womanist religious thought engage a variety of discourses; and (3) the importance of interreligious dialogue in womanist and ecowomanist discourse, thus breaking new ground and providing new entries into interfaith and interreligious dialogue about earth justice.

This chapter is therefore written from a third-wave womanist theoretical frame that features contemporary womanist discourse (discourse that centers the theological, religious, and ethical reflection of women of African descent and their interdisciplinary perspectives on religion) and shares dialogue across the African diaspora, making global links. In addition, the chapter engages interreligious dialogue and interdisciplinary methods that help to acknowledge, embrace, and examine the rich complexity of womanist religious thought.

There is an implicit assumption and myth in the traditional environmental movement that African Americans and other communities of color have little interest in earth justice, and that their numbers have been sorely lacking in the movement. The rationale often given to support such a claim is that African Americans and other communities of color are too often engaged in battles of social justice in an age of white supremacy. Facing the impact of unjust police brutality imparting fear into the rhythm of one's everyday existence, the constant pressure of having to prove the humanity and innate dignity of African peoples, and the reality of living in a culture wherein black women's bodies continue to be subjected to rape, shame, and even death at the hands of those who exercise social dominance is difficult *death-dealing* and life-transformative work.[3] In the midst of the urgency of cli-

---

[3] Emilie M. Townes, *Breaking the Fine Rain of Death: African Amer-*

mate change, however, many in activist communities have to fight for social justice in new and unexpected ways.

Considering the significance of the unjust treatment and exploitation of African Americans and the history of race and white supremacy in America, a scholar concerned about responsible cultural production of knowledge must ask the following question: Why is African American environmental history missing from the discourse of religion? This question might prompt additional questions: Has it been left out of the discourse intentionally? If so, why? Is the absence of African American environmental history an intentional move to reinforce particular racially biased beliefs pertaining to myths about the lack of African American intelligence, ability, humanity, or ethical sensibility? Is the absence designed to devalue the religious, cultural, and social protest thought that emerges from African American life, thus problematizing categories in Western discourse used to ignore these realities? Or rather is the absence of African American environmental history simply a problem of neglect? Or is it an unconscious *innocent* move of unknowing, perhaps based on an implicit bias that seems to repeatedly, systematically, and normatively ignore the history of race (and racism) in America and its connections to the environment?

However ill-founded or naïve the reasons for the absence of attention to African American environmental history (as well as the history of other peoples of color in the environmental movement) in the move toward recovering this history—and correcting the metanarrative that does not always acknowledge the significance and presence of this field—one must also be careful not to further silo African American environmental history as it is being developed. This move could result in the unhelpful effect of marginalizing all history about African Americans and the environment into one *subfield*,

ican Health Issues and a Womanist Ethic of Care (Eugene, OR: Wipf & Stock, 2006).

casting it into a lesser, or seemingly less valuable, discourse. It is important to acknowledge the important critical and creative thought necessary to develop theory and praxis in these fields. It is also important to engage the politics of the cultural production of knowledge in a way that insists on equity and historical accuracy, and serves to subvert the dominance of a false metanarrative that lacks racial and social consciousness but claims to be operating with good intentions.

In other words, there is an assumption within the discourse of environmental studies, and more specifically within the subfield of environmental religious ethics, that the history of African Americans, the civil rights movement, and such contemporary social movements as Black Lives Matter have little in common with concerns for earth justice. This assumption must be debunked if environmental ethics is to function in a true mode of justice. Social justice is connected to reflections on environmental degradation and should be considered vital for mainstream talk in religion and ecology.

This move not only widens the scope of environmental ethics but also invites the inclusion of theoretical frames that are non-Western and influenced by African, Asian, or indigenous cosmologies. The inclusion of such cosmologies and religious worldviews sheds new light on the perils of colonialism and its connection to environmental degradation. It helps us to recognize that African American environmental history is different and offers unique contributions to the wider discourse because it demands that the remnants of what African theologian Edward P. Antonio calls colonial ecology be acknowledged.[4] Too often traditional discourse in religion and ecology leaves out the important conversations that blend ethics, social justice, religion, racial consciousness, and ecology together. The

---

[4] Edward P. Antonio, "Ecology as Experience in African Indigenous Religions," in *Living Stones in the Household of God: The Legacy and Future of Black Theology*, ed. Linda E. Thomas, 146–57 (Minneapolis: Fortress Press, 2003).

development of African American environmental history, religious history, and ecowomanism suggests that these conversations must take place.

Having explained why and how African American environmental history, religious history, and ecowomanism engage religion and ecology, I now turn to a specific question. In light of the significant contributions and templates for social justice organizing that have emerged from the Black Lives Matter movement, are there specific antiracist reparations paradigms that can be translated for environmental justice paradigms and ecological reparations work? In this first section, I introduce African American environmental religious ethics and references of ecowomanism that have already been described in earlier chapters. The existence of these two fields fills a void in the traditional environmental movement and argues that, particularly when it comes to conversations about religion and ecology, African Americans and many communities of color have long been shepherding and guiding an important discourse that links social justice to earth justice by using an environmental justice paradigm.

Second, building on the third-wave womanist hallmark that recognizes global links and connections about religion, ecology, and gender across the African diaspora, this chapter explores how a frame for ecological reparations can be shaped from an ecowomanist African diasporic perspective. That is, I discuss parallels and intersections between racial and ecological reparations using an African diasporic lens. I conclude the chapter with remarks about the importance of uncovering African American religious and indigenous ecowisdom and environmental history for the development of ecological reparations in the face of climate change.

African American Environmental History

To date, there is limited focused research on the question of why African American environmental ethics has been left out of the discourse of religion and ecology.[5] In this section, I will focus on the history of the African American environmental justice movement in connection with the black church and the social protest tradition. This information provides a counternarrative to the metastory of the environmental movement that too often leaves out the histories and contributions of women and communities of color. This exploration begins by pointing to an important origin point in the work of Dr. Martin Luther King Jr. that makes the link between social and earth justice impossible to ignore.

As Dianne Glave highlights, the writings, preaching, and oratorical genius of King offered much more than a theoretical and theological foundation for black liberation theologies and contemporary perspectives on religion and the African diaspora.[6] King's work for social justice—and in particular his radical stance on love, the beloved community, and racial and economic justice—opened the doors for scholars, artists, everyday folk, and activists to get involved and raise consciousness about the gap between the haves and the have-nots. Interwoven within King's Christian understanding of redemptive suffering, divine justice, and unconditional love was a deep commitment to nonviolence and a belief in the innate dignity of all. King believed that if white Americans and people around the planet could overcome the myth of white racial superiority—if they could see and accept African Americans as fully human, as equally deserving of rights, humane treatment, and opportunity—their own morals would convince them to change public policy and laws that degraded persons of African descent. But as King records in many writings, speeches, and letters, includ-

[5] Willis Jennings, *The Future of Ethics: Sustainability, Social Justice and Religious Creativity* (Washington, DC: Georgetown University Press, 2013), 206–11.

[6] Dianne Glave, "Black Environmental Liberation Theology," in *To Love the Wind and the Rain: African Americans and Environmental History*, ed. Dianne Glave and Mark Stoll, 189–99 (Pittsburgh: University of Pittsburgh Press, 2006).

ing "Letter from a Birmingham Jail," King was often disappointed with white moderates whose political stance stopped short of taking a stance for justice and ending racial segregation. Too comfortable with the social power that white privilege presented to them, King became untrusting of white politicians as well as religious and community leaders who offered words of faith and reminders of Jesus's virtue of patience, but little action toward breaking the code of institutional racism.

Dispirited but still brave, King didn't stop. Moving beyond disappointment—and death threats—King expanded his scope of the civil rights movement to include not only *radical love* and racial justice, but also economic and environmental justice. King's passion for justice erupted past his theology as a Christian to include the religious orientation and economic status (or lack thereof) of others. That is, King was concerned, deeply concerned, about the poor and the oppressed.

This is precisely why King accepted a request to speak and organize on behalf of sanitation workers in Memphis, Tennessee, on April 3, 1968.[7] The Memphis movement exposed the deplorable conditions and environmental health hazards that workers had to face daily, all the while combating racism on the job. King grasped the connections between poverty, individual and institutional racism, and environmental health hazards, and he interpreted these links as threats to justice. These connections are not lost on many African American environmentalists. In fact, it is precisely this awareness of the links between race, class, gender, and environmental health that guides much of the research of scholars in environmental justice.[8] Coming from a

---

[7] Melanie L. Harris, "Ecowomanism: An Introduction," *Worldviews: Global Religions, Culture, and Ecology* 20, no. 1 (2016): 5–14.

[8] For example, Robert Bullard, *Dumping in Dixie: Race, Class and Environmental Quality* (Boulder, CO: Westview Press, 2000); Dorceta E. Taylor, "Race, Class, Gender, and American Environmentalism," United States Department of Agriculture Forest Service Pacific Northwest Research Station General Technical Report PNW-GTR-534, April 2002; and Florence Margai, *Environmental Health Hazards and Social Justice:*

variety of disciplines, including sociology, geography, and religion, these scholars also signal an important theoretical frame and approach to investigating environmental injustice, climate violence, and environmental racism. The work of historians and literary artists such as Kimberly K. Smith,[9] Kimberly N. Ruffin,[10] and Camille T. Dungy[11] also points to the significant contributions to the field of environmental studies coming from people of African descent who have been forced to confront systems of economic, gender, and racial oppression.

The environmental justice paradigm links environmental concern with a social justice agenda attuned to the connections between environmental health hazards and race, class, and gender disparities.[12] The environmental justice paradigm is illustrated by acts of justice modeled by King; black church women protesting toxic waste dumping in North Carolina, New Orleans, and New York City; the work of the National Association for the Advancement of Colored People; and leaders such as Dorothy Height and contemporary leaders such as Majora Carter. The paradigm provides a foundation for both theoretical and praxis-oriented approaches that help expand traditional environmental paradigms of *conservation* or *preservation*. This expansion helps the discourse recognize the impact of historical and contemporary realities (such as a rise in racial violence) as well as the cumulative impact that structural forms of environmental injustice can have on *earthling* communities and communities of faith.

Geographical Perspectives on Race and Class Disparities (Washington, DC: Earthscan, 2010).

[9] Kimberly K. Smith, *African American Environmental Thought: Foundations* (Kansas City: University Press of Kansas, 2007).

[10] Kimberly N. Ruffin, *Black on Earth: African American Ecoliterary Traditions* (Athens: University of Georgia Press, 2010).

[11] Camille T. Dungy, *Black Nature: Four Centuries of African American Nature Poetry* (Athens: University of Georgia Press, 2009).

[12] Dorceta E. Taylor, *Toxic Communities: Environmental Racism, Industrial Pollution, and Residential Mobility* (New York: New York University Press, 2014).

African and African American Environmental Religious Ethics

Far from absent from the struggle, African Americans have been on the journey for justice, and earth justice, since—some would argue before—being forcibly brought to North American shores on the slave ships from Africa. While arguments from political theorists and historians might place the origins of African American environmentalism at the start of black agrarianism, during the height of the transatlantic slave trade, or in the midst of Jim and Jane Crow, a disciplinary lens from religion suggests that the origins of African American environmentalism lie in a history much deeper than that: in the heart of African cosmology.

African cosmology connects the realms of spirit, nature, and humanity into one flowing web of life. That is, instead of a hierarchal or dualistic structure, African cosmology functions in a circular manner emphasizing interconnectedness and, in the words of Thich Nhat Hanh, "interbeing."[13] It is important to note that I am intentionally making connections between Asian and African cosmologies, and I argue that the worldviews and perspectives on earth ethics that emerge from these cosmologies shed new light on environmental justice. These perspectives from communities of color are necessary in the movement as we face down climate change.

As has been argued by religious scholars including John Mbiti,[14] Peter Paris,[15] Barbara Holmes,[16] and others, an African cosmological perspective drastically changes one's perspective of earth care or environmental justice because in fact a

---

[13] Thich Nhat Hanh, *The Heart of Understanding: Commentaries on the Prajnaparamita Heart Sutra* (Berkeley, CA: Parallax Press, 1998).

[14] John S. Mbiti, *Introduction to African Religion,* 2nd ed. (Long Grove, IL: Waveland Press, 2015).

[15] Peter J. Paris, *The Spirituality of African Peoples: The Search for a Common Moral Landscape* (Minneapolis: Fortress Press, 1995).

[16] Barbara Holmes, *Race and Cosmos: An Invitation to View the World Differently* (New York: Bloomsbury T & T Clark, 2002).

being, or human being, is understood to be a vital part, but not the center, of the universe. That is, these cosmologies lend themselves toward seeing the earth as fully and intimately connected. "Everything is everything" is one hip-hop phrase whose signified meaning connotes this kind of interconnectedness.[17] As such, African cosmology also promotes a kind of innate ethical message to care for the planet. In addition to the ancestral spiritual connections that must be honored according to many African religious traditions, an ethical mandate to care for the earth is often communicated from African cosmologies because of the interconnectedness. To care for the earth is to care for the self and vice versa.

This kind of cosmology serves as a base from which African American environmental ethics and ecowomanism grow. Both these fields honor and operate in ways that evoke the same kind of interconnectedness in African cosmology and understand this to be a central value (such as the value of community) in womanist thought, and in African and black life. The community, and herein the earth community, is important to keep in balance. Honoring this balance is also reflected in relationships between human and nonhuman beings. That is, African cosmology deeply shapes the ethical mores of how one ought to care for the earth, and sheds light on how individual humans ought to act toward the earth and each other in communion. This kind of *earth ethic* that emerges from African cosmology has deeply influenced forms of black liberation theology and womanist religious thought. This can be seen most clearly in the work of eco-theologians Theo Walker,[18] Karen Baker-Fletcher,[19] and

---

[17] Lauryn Hill, *Everything Is Everything*, Sony, 1999, CD.

[18] Theodore Walker, "African-American Resources for More Inclusive Liberation Theology," in *Good News for Animals? Christian Approaches to Animal Well-Being*, ed. C. Pinches and J. B. McDaniel, 163–71 (Maryknoll, NY: Orbis Books, 1993).

[19] Karen Baker-Fletcher, *Sisters of Dust, Sisters of Spirit: Womanist Wordings on God and Creation* (Minneapolis: Fortress Press, 1998).

Emilie M. Townes.[20] Of particular note, Delores S. Williams's essay "Sin, Nature and Black Women's Bodies"[21] (a foundational resource for ecowomanism) argues that there is a connection between the logic of domination present in white supremacy, colonial Christianity, and sexist ideology that sanctioned the objectification of black enslaved women's bodies during slavery (and since). Drawing on the work of several pioneering woman-ist thinkers and theologians, James H. Cone draws direct links between black liberation theology and ecological justice:

> The logic that led to slavery and segregation in the Americas, colonialization and apartheid in Africa, and the rule of white supremacy throughout the world is the same one that leads to the exploitation of animals and the ravaging of nature. . . . People who fight against white racism but fail to connect it to the degradation of the earth are anti-ecological—whether they know it or not. People who struggle against environmental degradation but do not incorporate in it a disciplined and sustained fight against white supremacy are rac-ists—whether they know it or not. The fight for justice cannot be segregated but must be integrated with the fight for life in all its forms.[22]

Recognizing the links within the logic of oppression that have negatively impacted peoples of color, and peoples of African descent throughout the diaspora, Cone's argument points us back to the important source that African cosmology is for

---

[20] Townes, *Breaking the Fine Rain of Death*.

[21] Delores S. Williams, "Sin, Nature and Black Women's Bodies," in *Ecofeminism and the Sacred*, ed. Carol Adams, 24–29 (New York: Continuum, 1993).

[22] James H. Cone, "Whose Earth Is It Anyway?" in *Earth Habitat: Eco-Justice and the Church's Response*, ed. Dieter Hessel and Larry Rasmussen, 23–32 (Minneapolis: Fortress Press, 2001).

developing the discourse of black liberation theology, religion, and ecology, and especially ecowomanism.

Ecowomanism: A Review

As has been explained in previous chapters, ecowomanism is a critical reflection and contemplation on environmental justice from a womanist perspective and, more specifically, from the perspectives of African and indigenous women. It links a social justice agenda to environmental justice and recognizes the similar logic of domination at work in parallel oppressions suffered by women and the earth. That is, just as women of color have historically suffered multiple forms of oppression, including racism, classism, sexism, and heterosexism, so has the earth suffered due to debasing and devaluing attitudes about the earth that suggest that nonhuman beings (earth) have less status and worth than human beings. Regrettably, this kind of anthropocentric attitude has resulted in many human cultures adopting hierarchal values and dualisms that have resulted in the Anthropocene: a new geological epoch, and many would argue a new climate age, resulting from the impact human life and lifestyle have had on the planet.

As a discourse that blends methods from environmental studies and womanist religious thought and ethics, ecowomanism offers unique gifts to the wider field in that it highlights the contributions that women of African descent and indigenous women have made to the environmental justice movement. Ecowomanism also examines how their theological voices and ethical perspectives contribute new strategies of earth justice. Noting the paradoxical historical relationship that African American women have had with the earth (i.e., being named as property the same as the earth, and devalued in similar ways as the earth) in the midst of surviving a white supremacist society, ecowomanism pays attention to the complex subjectivity of African American women. The approach uses multilayered analysis to investigate earth justice in a way that honors the biodiversity of the earth, while also honoring varied particular experiences of African American women as human beings living in the earth community. Using intersectional analysis when approaching earth justice, ecowomanism is a lens that contributes solutions to the ecological crisis that we are living in today, by connecting the agenda of social justice with earth justice or, in other words, by developing a theological liberationist social justice agenda—moving toward race, class, gender, and sexual justice, while also lifting up earth justice.

As noted in the work of celebrated cultural geologist Florence Margai,[23] sociologist Dorceta E. Taylor,[24] and others, the connection between race and class and environmental health disparities can no longer be ignored. Ecowomanism joins the conversation, inviting reflection on the inner lives of women environmental activists, the spiritual practices of those who practice environmental justice, as well as the communities of faith and encouragement that instill and reinforce their values for earth justice with hope.

Making Connections:
African Religion, Ecology, and the Diaspora

Before moving forward to discuss more about the contributions of ecowomanism, it is important to nuance the understanding of African cosmology and an ecowomanist adoption of it. Most thinkers would consider it a risk to ground a concept and method, such as ecowomanism, into a cultural frame rather than a historical frame. One disadvantage, for example, of claiming that womanist race–class–gender analysis is central to ecowomanist method and approaches is that it places

---

[23] Florence Margai, *Environmental Health Hazards and Social Justice: Geographical Perspectives on Race and Class Disparities* (Washington, DC: Earthscan, 2010).

[24] Dorceta E. Taylor, *The Environment and the People in American Cities, 1600s–1900s: Disorder, Inequality and Social Change* (Durham, NC: Duke University Press, 2009).

ecowomanism in the center of a debate about identity politics, at best, and exhibits the impact of colonial ecology, at worst. That is, without the presence of racial hierarchies, metanarratives that leave out communities of color, and other structural oppressions, some argue there would be no need for a womanist or ecowomanist approach. Black and womanist theologies and ethics have been interpreted as reactionary responses to traditional (read: white) theologies and therefore suspect in that their theoretical base may in fact be based on the same theory used by the oppressors. Using the master's tools to dismantle the master's house, to paraphrase Audre Lorde,[25] is a difficult quandary and debate that many black liberation and womanist theologians, ethicists, and theorists have engaged.

Another contentious element in ecowomanist theory involves its adoption of an African cosmological frame. Antonio,[26] Rose Mary Amenga-Etego,[27] and other African traditional religion scholars argue that Western religious, anthropological, and even cultural lenses have misframed the relations between African traditional religions and ecology in problematic ways. This is important because womanist ethics has often been labeled a Western enterprise, and ecowomanism could be (mis)understood the same way. Although I do not agree with this characterization and maintain that womanist religious thought and ecowomanism both attempt to be shaped by nondualistic and nonhierarchal thinking, it is worth noting this very important debate.

Many scholars of African traditional and indigenous religion argue that African traditional religions are too often misunderstood and misinterpreted due to a colonial impetus within

---

[25] Audre Lorde, "The Master's Tools Will Never Dismantle the Master's House," in *Sister Outsider: Essays and Speeches* (Berkeley, CA: Crossing Press, 1984), 110–14.

[26] Antonio, "Ecology as Experience in African Indigenous Religions."

[27] Rose Mary Amenga-Etego, *Mending the Broken Pieces: Indigenous Religion and Sustainable Rural Development in Northern Ghana* (Trenton, NJ: World Press, 2011).

most Western lenses. For example, Antonio warns of the Western colonial influence on ecological discourse by problematizing the assumptions that many religious thinkers in the West make about African people and worldviews. In Antonio's view, the claim that Africans are closer to nature and therefore their worldviews have within them practices that are more earth-honoring than European practices and theologies of nature is wrong and constructed on a false premise. This Western assumption is, at best, culturally unaware and, at worst, racist.

Antonio critiques malformed assumptions often made by white and European environmentalists and exposes their deep investment in a logic that attempts to control Africans and African worldviews. Noting how the logic of domination has woven through the history of colonization and crippled the earth, Antonio points to the eerie similarity between colonial moves to control the bodies of Africans and the body of the earth. He asks whether the white and European assumption that Africans are closer to nature and their move to point their scholarly arrows back toward African religious roots for answers about climate change is authentic or an odd act of repentance for the construction of colonial ecology. His essay prompts ecowomanist scholars to ask the question forthrightly: is the move back to African religion, the adoption of African cosmology, and the over-romanticizing of the very nature, culture, and values of Africanness (i.e., blackness) actually an odd act of repentance—a conceptual move toward some form (however misshapen) of ecological reparations?

In the frantic urgency of climate change, environmentalists of every discourse are often left scrambling, ready to pounce and exploit the very blackness and African cosmological connection embedded in African indigenous religions for the sake of saving their own (colonial) ecological home (or their *ecological souls*). As the history of colonialism proves, there is a connection between exploiting African peoples and their lands, and this logic of domination has had a major impact on our current climate crisis. Colonization is one of the reasons for climate injustice; therefore, social justice is directly related to climate or earth justice. Social justice is earth justice. Earth justice is social justice.

Dialogue with theologians and African religious scholars, such as Antonio, turns the ecowomanist's gaze into herself for self-reflection and critique. Similar to the methodological move of self-reflection gleaned from the work of womanist ethicists, Antonio's point invites ecowomanism to more closely analyze its structures and moral foundations. By starting with African cosmology as a base from which to honor African, African American, and indigenous voices of women and their contributions to environmental justice, is ecowomanism casting itself into the long shadow of colonization? Is it practicing colonial ecology?

I say no. Ecowomanism honors its African cosmological roots as a valid and authentic epistemology of how to be an ethical earthling, living on the planet today. As many African peoples' values are shaped by their religion and religious practice, so, too, are ecowomanism's values shaped by their identity as descendants of Africa, carrying embodied and actual indigenous roots. To honor African cosmologies—and the theories and practices of environmental justice that are informed by them—is an act and method of resistance in that it joins the postcolonial move to expose the remnants of colonial ecology and dismantle this by infusing the field with true ecowomanist epistemology. Womanist earth stories, African American agricultural knowledge, and African ethical worldviews model interconnectedness and help us honor the earth and live faithfully on the planet with others.

"I Can't Breathe"

Following the death of Eric Garner—an African American man who was killed on July 17, 2014, in New York City at the hands of a police officer who used an illegal choke hold to pin him down to the ground, ignoring his pleas of "I can't breathe,

I can't breathe"—I, like many environmental activists, took a step back. Black Lives Matter had grown into a movement, and many scholars, activists, teachers, and religious leaders were taking to the streets to protest the rise in racial violence. Clearly black women and men were being targeted. Calling on the wisdom of Ida B. Wells, whose *A Red Record* exposed the horrors of white supremacist lynching of black women and men across the United States for three gruesome years, and examining the roots of white supremacy and its connections to forms of Christianity that normatively ignore social justice as a base from which to do theology, I began to take a long view of the work of justice being done in the green movement. The autopsy performed by the coroner in New York revealed that Eric Garner did not only suffer from the impact of the illegal choke hold forced on him by the officer; Eric Garner also had asthma. As a consequence of the environmental health hazard of air pollution in Staten Island, Eric Garner, like thousands of children and adults living in and breathing in nonclean air, suffered not only because of racially motivated violence, but also because the air in his community robbed him of a normal quality of life: the right to breathe clean. The crescendoing call that many of us are hearing now is a call for all of us to use an environmental justice paradigm, to see the connections between social justice and environmental justice, and to hear these important earth stories. African American environmental history and herstory has never been so important. Its riches, contributions, stories, and solutions have never before been so valuable for the work of justice.

CHAPTER FOUR

Engaging Transformation: Ecowomanist Spirituality

This chapter builds on an ecowomanist method by engaging transformation in the fifth step. This step introduces different forms of ecowomanist spirituality as embodied practices of spiritual activism for environmental justice. These forms of activism are unique in that they are informed by ecowomanist values and principles. Woven from the fabric of womanist religious thought and ecowomanist discourse, ecowomanist spirituality acknowledges parallels between the unjust treatment of women of African descent and the unjust treatment of the body of the earth. Similar to womanist thought, and reflective of womanist ethics, ecowomanist spirituality is upheld by overarching themes of justice, prophetic wisdom, and the sacredness of earth. Since theory and praxis are connected in womanist and ecowomanist thought, this chapter also explores spiritual activism as a base for conceptualizing ecowomanist thought and practicing environmental justice.

Spiritual activism is described best by womanist scholar and ecowomanist writer Layli Maparyan as "social or ecological transformational activity rooted in a spiritual belief system or set of spiritual practices. . . . Spiritual activism is putting spirituality to work for positive social and ecological change."[1] Since human, social, and cultural transformation is necessary for social change and justice work, transformation is a natural output of ecowomanist work and study. That is, transformation is not only a step in ecowomanist method but also a valuable step in ecowomanist spiritual activism.

The focus on engaging transformation as the fifth methodological step can be seen through the exploration of the spiritual activism of ecowomanist activists, scholars, and writers. For the purpose of this work, we will focus on the work of three ecowomanists who joined together to promote the work and scholarship of ecowomanism by publishing together in a special issue on *Ecowomanism: Earth-Honoring Faiths.*[2]

The issue features essays written by Rose Mary Amenga-Etego, Xiumei Pu, Layli Maparyan, Sofia Betancourt, Valdina Oliveria Pinto, Rachel E. Harding, Mercy Oduyoye, and myself. In this chapter, I will focus on the scholarly essays authored by Amenga-Etego and Oduyoye. By focusing on these models of ecowomanist spirituality, this chapter serves to further the published conversation and highlight the unique resources across the African diaspora, inclusive of interfaith and interreligious perspectives of ecowomanism. In this way the chapter intentionally points toward the significance of interreligious thought within ecowomanism, crafting a path toward the last two steps of the method: These are step six, sharing interfaith and interreligious dialogue among ecowomanist earth-honoring faiths, and step seven, taking action for earth justice through teaching and pedagogy.

Alice Walker is, in many ways, the *ecowomanist mother* whose work and writings set an important conceptual frame for development of ecowomanist thought and activism. As such, in addition to a focus on models of ecowomanist spirituality in

---

[1] Layli Maparyan, *The Womanist Idea* (New York: Routledge, 2012), 119.

[2] Christopher Key Chapple and Melanie L. Harris (guest editor), *Worldviews: Global Religions, Culture, and Ecology* 20, no. 1 (2016): 1–101.

the essays, this chapter will also examine the work and writings of Walker as a model of ecowomanist spirituality. Following a brief introduction to the work of Walker and the emergence of ecowomanist spirituality, I will begin to explore the various models of ecowomanist spirituality in the featured essays by posing two questions, which provide an arc and structure for the analysis of each ecowomanist's work. The two questions that serve to guide the exploration into ecowomanist spirituality are (1) How are African and African American women's practices of ecowomanist spirituality and earth-honoring faiths illustrated in their religions or religious commitments, and (2) How do these forms of ecowomanist spirituality simultaneously influence spiritual activism? The work of each ecowomanist reveals the uniqueness of each earth-honoring faith and attempts to uncover why and how each author identifies as an ecowomanist willing to speak in the prophetic tone of ecowomanism at this time. We begin with Walker's reflections on the model of ecowomanist spirituality.

Alice Walker

A renowned literary writer, literary artist, and committed activist, Alice Walker is the first African American woman writer to ever receive the Pulitzer Prize.[3] Her book *The Color Purple* has received numerous prestigious awards and has across the decades been heralded as one of literature's most important classics. As discussed above, her work and sensibilities to environmental justice are central points in the work of ecowomanist spirituality, since her work both grounds theory for the field as well as models ecowomanist activism. This can be seen most clearly in essays she has written, including "Everything Is

---

[3] This section builds on the author's previous work, "Alice Walker and the Emergence of Ecowomanist Spirituality," in *Spirit and Nature: The Study of Christian Spirituality in a Time of Ecological Urgency*, ed. Timothy Hessell-Robinson and Ray Maria McNamara, 220–36 (Eugene, OR: Pickwick, Princeton Theological Monograph Series, 2011).

a Human Being" and "Nuclear Madness," and throughout her volumes of essays, including *We Are the Ones We Have Been Waiting For* and *The Cushion in the Road*.[4]

A glance at the titles of ecowomanist writings referenced above reveals the significance of Walker's life of activism and writings for ecowomanism. Many of the theorists mentioned above glean values, strategies for earth-justice activism, and inspiration from Walker. In particular, Walker's sense of activism is of primary importance in that it arises from her love for the earth and her love and belief in humanity. She describes this briefly in her introduction of the nonfiction collection of essays *Anything We Love Can Be Saved: A Writer's Activism*.[5] Here she describes the two foundational principles that guide justice movements, saying,

> During my years of being close to people engaged in changing the world I have seen fear turn into courage. Sorrow into joy. Funerals into celebrations. Because whatever the consequences, people, standing side by side, have expressed who they really are, and that ultimately they believe in the love of the world and each other enough to be that—which is the foundation of activism.[6]

Love of the world (read: earth) and a love of one another (read: humanity) are the two foundations of activism for

---

[4] Alice Walker, "Everything Is a Human Being," in *Living by the Word: Selected Writings 1973–1987* (New York: Harcourt Brace Jovanovich, 1988), 139–52; Alice Walker, "Nuclear Madness: What You Can Do," in *In Search of Our Mothers' Gardens: Womanist Prose* (New York: Harcourt Brace Jovanovich, 1983), 343–46; Alice Walker, *We Are the Ones We Have Been Waiting For: Inner Light in a Time of Darkness* (New York: New Press, 2006); Alice Walker, *The Cushion in the Road: Meditation and Wandering as the Whole World Awakens to Being in Harm's Way* (New York: New Press, 2013).

[5] Alice Walker, "Introduction," in *Anything We Love Can Be Saved: A Writer's Activism* (New York: Random House, 1997), xxii.

[6] Ibid.

Walker, and according to her writings both are rooted in a sense that everyone (i.e., all of humanity) and everything (i.e., every nonhuman being) is safe. She locates this understanding in her experience of community as a child growing up in Georgia, and in the moral life and sensibilities of her mother. She writes that the type of love that informs activism reflects "my mother's love of beauty, the well-tended garden and the carefully swept yard, [and] her satisfaction in knowing everyone in her environment was sheltered and fed."[7] In essence, the assurance of communal well-being, the value of mutual love, and respect of the earth support an ethical imperative for earth justice in Walker's work. It is this sense of earth-justice activism that motivates ecowomanist writers, environmental activists, and ecologists to challenge the status quo and draw on Walker's work to help make humanity more aware of the state of the environment.

In such essays as "Nuclear Madness,"[8] "The Universe Responds: Or, How I Learned We Can Have Peace on Earth,"[9] and "Only Justice Can Stop a Curse,"[10] Walker's ethical imperative and deep concern for the earth shine clearly as she gives examples of ecological disasters; explains how they impact the life of the earth, as well as human life; and urgently appeals to readers to get involved in the environmental movement. One example of how she does this is found in "Nuclear Madness: What You Can Do."[11] In this book review of Helen Caldicott's book, Walker praises the author for providing helpful analysis and attempting to answer the question of why people have stopped becoming active in the environmental justice movement. Walker writes in urgent tones to encourage readers to

---

[7] Ibid., xxiv.

[8] Walker, "Nuclear Madness."

[9] Alice Walker, "The Universe Responds: Or, How I Learned We Can Have Peace on Earth," in *Living by the Word*, 187–93.

[10] Alice Walker, "Only Justice Can Stop a Curse," in *In Search of Our Mothers' Gardens*, 338–42.

[11] Walker, "Nuclear Madness."

become active in the antinuclear save-the-earth movement. Personifying the earth as a mother with universal status and drawing connections between racism as an oppression suffered by people of color and potential nuclear action as an oppression suffered by the earth, Walker writes, "The good news may be that Nature is phasing out the white man, but the bad news is that's who She [Mother Earth] thinks we all are."[12] The connection between racism and earth injustice that Walker implies indicates that she is aware of a link between injustices: in this case, racial injustice and earth injustice.

For ecowomanism, this suggests that oppressions are connected, and Walker's analysis reinforces the need for womanist intersectional analysis in order to see the damning effects earth injustice can have on people of color, the earth, and *all* people living with the earth.

"Nuclear Madness"[13] is also an example of how Walker attempts to boost interest and make people of color more aware of their important role in the environmental movement. Earlier in the essay Walker points out that while the earth or environmental movement is traditionally known as a *white persons'* movement, there is a deep connection between the abuse of the earth and the abuse of people of color. "Individuals must join others. No time to quibble about survival being 'a white issue.' No time to claim you don't live here, too," she writes. This is similar to the ways that Dorceta E. Taylor raises the issue of racial inclusion in an April 2002 US Forest Service document[14] and black theologian James H. Cone writes of the importance of race analysis for environmental ethics.[15]

---

12 Ibid., 146.

13 Ibid.

14 Dorceta E. Taylor, "Race, Class, Gender, and American Environmentalism," United States Department of Agriculture Forest Service Pacific Northwest Research Station General Technical Report PNW-GTR-534, April 2002.

15 James H. Cone, "Whose Earth Is It Anyway?" in *Earth Habitat:*

Another important essay by Walker that illustrates eco-womanist thought is "Everything Is a Human Being."[16] Here Walker expands on the theme of humanization, and the fact that all humans ought to receive equal treatment, to include an equality of beings. She suggest that honor, agency, and worth ought to be extended to parts of nature so that trees, birds, lakes, rivers, mountains, and streams existing in *safe* sanctuaries, such as public parks, cannot be torn down and polluted. In the same way that she and countless others fought for human and civil rights for African Americans in this country, here she draws a parallel between the impact of white supremacy to devalue African Americans in American history and the history and practice of devaluing earth in a global capitalized system.

In the essay, she also argues that the wisdom offered by Native American spiritualities is important in that it sees the connection between people (humans) and the earth. In comparing the detrimental effects of logging in California to the cutting down of "old sisters and brothers," Walker notes the relational nature between herself as a human and the trees. In grieving tones she writes, "I saw the loggers' trucks, like enormous hearses, carrying the battered bodies of the old sisters and brothers, as I thought of them, down to the lumberyards in the valley. . . . It was of this endless funeral procession that I thought as I lay across the feet of the sick old relatives whose 'safe' existence in a public park (away from logging trucks) had not kept them safe at all."[17]

By drawing a familial connection between the trees and humans, Walker insists that everything—all creatures, all nature, and all humans—be treated more humanely. She writes that humans must "restore the Earth," pointing to "its dignity

---

Eco-Justice and the Church's Response, ed. Dieter Hessel and Larry Rasmussen, 23–32 (Minneapolis: Fortress Press, 2001), 23–32.

[16] Walker, "Everything Is a Human Being."

[17] Ibid., 141.

as a living being," and only by doing this will humans realize their own intimate connection with the earth and with their own humanity. According to Walker, being accountable for and to the earth is a moral imperative for one operating within an understanding that the earth, nature, divinity, and humanity are interrelated.

Walker's writing and sense of activism are not the only elements that serve as a theoretical base for ecowomanism. Her definition of *womanist*, as well as the religious school of thought inspired by the term, also serves as the theoretical and metaphorical scaffolding that frames ecowomanist thought.

The Definition of *Womanist*: Center of Ecowomanist Thought

Although womanist thought is commonly identified with celebrating religious perspectives,[18] ideas, and theological constructs that help African-descended women understand, survive, and live fully into their complex subjectivity, the term *womanist* is not simply a religious term. In fact, *womanist*, as defined by Walker,[19] reflects many different aspects of ecowomanist spirituality, and of being and surviving as an African-descended woman in a global context. While it does celebrate the *Spirit* and highlight the important place spiritualities and faith systems have in the lives of women of African

---

[18] Though there is obvious reference to the religious or spiritual in the definition of *womanist*, it is important to point out that the definition does not promote a certain religious tradition over any other. Nor does it condemn any religious tradition that is life affirming and life giving to African-descended women. In essence, womanist spirituality, and therefore the basis of womanist religious thought, values all religious traditions that uphold the characteristics of being a womanist and promote intersectional race, class, and gender analysis in order to reveal moral codes, survival strategies, and life techniques that enhance the fullness of life for African-descended women.

[19] Walker, *In Search of Our Mothers' Gardens*, xi.

descent, the definition also illustrates the various political, ecological, racial, gender, class, and sexual identities that women live into every day.

Similar to a traditional dictionary format, Walker's definition of *womanist*[20] is divided into four parts, dictating several different characteristics of a womanist. The first part identifies *womanist* with black feminism and feminisms of color.[21] Reference is made to the significance of mother-to-daughter relationships in this part of the definition, and it alludes to the cultural practice of honoring one's elders—a practice considered normative among younger and older African American women in the southern United States.[22] The saying, "You acting wom-

---

[20] Ibid.

[21] For additional conversation about the distinctions between black feminism and womanism, see Traci C. West, "Is a Womanist a Black Feminist? Marking the Distinctions and Defying Them: A Black Feminist Response," in *Deeper Shades of Purple: Womanism in Religion and Society*, ed. Stacey Floyd-Thomas, 291–95 (New York: New York University Press, 2006). It is also notable that several feminists of color have identified with the term *womanist*. See Baker-Fletcher and Baker-Fletcher's discussion of this in *My Sister, My Brother* (Eugene, OR: Wipf and Stock, 2002), 5.

[22] It is important to note that Walker comes from the southern United States and is heavily influenced by this cultural background. According to Evelyn C. White's biography, *Alice Walker: A Life* (New York: W. W. Norton, 2004), Walker was raised in an all-black community in Georgia, and this experience is sewn into her definition of *womanist*. Questions about whether it is appropriate for scholars to reference the term *womanist* or not, because of its regional connection, have been raised by such scholars as Monica A. Coleman in the roundtable discussion essay "Must I Be a Womanist?" *Journal of Feminist Studies in Religion* 22, no. 1 (2006): 85–134. In conversation with many other womanist and black feminist scholars, Coleman raises a question about whether an African American female religious scholar must identify as a womanist, simply because of her racial and gender identity, and whether a womanist must share the values, culture, and experiences familiar to those whose own sense of womanism is influenced by cultural practices of the southern United States. In keeping with the womanist value of self-naming and agency of a woman to name

anish" (i.e., like a woman) is used as a signifying phrase with at least a double meaning. Signifying can best be described as an African American folk hermeneutic used to elicit multiple meanings from texts, phrases, and symbols that may not be directly apparent. It also involves encoding messages or meanings into text, phrases, symbols, and the like. According to African American religious scholar Theophus Smith, author of the landmark text *Conjuring Culture*,[23] the act of signifying is done in a gamelike fashion by coming up with multiple meanings of a text beyond the original meaning, manipulating the various meanings by reinterpreting them, and forming a counterinterpretation of the same text.[24] The phrase "you acting womanish" in the womanist definition is an example of signification in that there are two meanings of the phrase implied in the definition. The first meaning serves as a disciplinary or corrective statement that reminds the younger women of their cultural *place* in the hierarchal order of members of a certain communal group.[25]

---

herself as she sees fit, I argue that one does not have to be from the region, nor should one feel forced to take on a set of African American southern values in order to identify as a womanist.

[23] Theophus H. Smith, *Conjuring Culture: Biblical Formations of Black America* (New York: Oxford University Press, 1994).

[24] The way in which the newly constructed meanings of the text are developed can be viewed as a way of *outwitting* the originator of the original text. As such, signifying is used as a device, within black religious/womanist thought and cultural theory, to promote an understanding of a *text within a text*. It encourages the close study of the different ways black peoples have reinterpreted and reenvisioned new meanings of text that were originally intended to dehumanize them and shows the genius of black thought to transform the very same text to carry meanings of survival, freedom, and empowerment.

[25] Traditionally, in African American southern culture, the younger one is expected to exhibit less agency and concede to the will or decision of the elder. While this is true, it is important to note the major contributions of young African American teens and children who exhibited their agency

However, the phrase also connotes a second meaning. This second meaning directly counters the first in that it promotes the agency of the younger to act, to be, and to strive to live into a greater source of strength, wisdom, and power as a woman—even before she has reached the culturally appropriate time or accepted age. The list of characteristics that Walker uses to represent a womanist includes the following: "outrageous," "audacious," and "courageous." Each of these connotes agency onto the recipient and also suggests a counternormative attitude taken on by the womanist. The interest in constructing epistemologies is also reflected in this first part of the definition, since a womanist is seen as "wanting to know more and in greater depth than is considered 'good' for one."[26]

The second part of the *womanist* definition refers to relationality and relationship to community, partners, family, culture, and society. It begins by celebrating a woman's sexual being and identity with a description that supports the love shared between women, sexual and nonsexual.[27] This part of

---

forthrightly during the civil rights movement in the United States. Teenage students involved in SNCC and children involved in children's marches in Georgia and throughout the South are examples of how this culturally accepted norm has been challenged for the sake of social justice. See the documentary film *Eyes on the Prize* and *Hope and History: Why We Must Share the Story of the Movement* by Vincent Harding (New York: Orbis Books, 1990) for more information.

[26] The construction of womanist epistemologies is a primary theme in M. Shawn Copeland's understanding of the work of womanism as explicated in her essay "A Thinking Margin: The Womanist Movement as Critical Cognitive Praxis," in Floyd-Thomas, *Deeper Shades of Purple*, 226–35. Also see Linda E. Thomas, "Womanist Theology, Epistemology, and a New Anthropological Paradigm," *CrossCurrents* 48, no. 4 (Winter 1998): 488–99.

[27] Important discourse on sexuality and womanist religious thought can be found in the groundbreaking work by such womanists as Kelly Brown Douglas in *Sexuality in the Black Church: A Womanist Perspective* (Maryknoll, NY: Orbis Books, 1999) and *What's Faith Got to Do with It: Black Bodies/Christian Souls* (Maryknoll, NY: Orbis Books,

the definition also celebrates the love shared between women and men, sexual and nonsexual. Women's culture, women's emotional flexibility, and women's strength are highlighted as central themes in part two of the definition and suggests that these are not only characteristics of womanists but also everyday virtues embodied by most women, even though they are not always celebrated in patriarchal societies. One of the clearest ethical imperatives in the entire definition of *womanist* is found in the second part, pointing to the commitment a womanist exemplifies to the "survival and wholeness of entire people, male *and* female." The significance of the italics that Walker adds to the word "and" in the last fragment between the words *male* and *female* suggests that for Walker, at the time that she was constructing the *womanist* definition, a clear statement needed to be made about the necessity of both women and men to be involved in the justice-seeking work of womanism. As an active participant in the civil rights movement and one who shared a deep commitment to the work and vision of Martin Luther King Jr. and Coretta Scott King, Walker's commitment to a gender-inclusive justice movement underscores the focus of the womanist community to be the goal of liberation for all humans and the earth. While womanism certainly praises communities established and maintained by and for women, it does not exclude men to the point of *male-bashing*. This is important in light of the fact that at the time that Walker was constructing the definition of *womanist*,

---

2005); Renee Leslie Hill, "Who Are We for Each Other? Sexism, Sexuality and Womanist Theology," in *Black Theology: A Documentary History, volume 2: 1980–1992*, ed. James H. Cone and Gayraud S. Wilmore, 345–51 (Maryknoll, NY: Orbis Books, 1993), as well as in the work of black feminist social ethicist Traci C. West, *Disruptive Christian Ethics: When Racism and Women's Lives Matter* (Louisville, KY: Westminster John Knox Press, 2006), and *Wounds of the Spirit: Black Women, Violence, and Resistance Ethics* (New York: New York University Press, 1996); and in the work of many others writing from both black feminist and womanist perspectives.

many strains of white feminism being practiced were vehemently opposed to allowing men to participate in the feminist movement. The emphasis on both community and wholeness in the second part of the *womanist* definition points to Walker's value of community, and wholeness for all, including all genders; thus, the definition of *womanist* is gender inclusive.

Part two of the definition is also political in nature in that it suggests that sometimes women of African descent and their communities need to separate themselves from the larger majority-white culture in order to rewater their roots and rediscover what makes them unique. This gives them time to remind themselves that despite the awful historical atrocities of racism, classism, sexism, and heterosexism, African-descended people are still beautifully human in their own sight and in the sight of God. This part also acknowledges the differences between people included in a womanist community, especially regarding color. Walker's inclusion of a fictive conversation between a mother and daughter in this part of the definition not only lifts up the necessity of acknowledging the presence of colorism in African-descended peoples' culture and community, but also brings forth the first reference to nature in the *womanist* definition.

The flower garden, "with every color flower represented," is a metaphorical image that Walker uses to note the inclusion of various skin tones, hues, and colors of African-descended people in the womanist community. This image is also reflective of Walker's own attention to nature. The natural presence of flowers shows up here in the *womanist* definition and throughout Walker's writings.[28] It is because of the prevalence

---

[28] See Walker's reference to her mother's joy of gardening in "In Search of Our Mothers' Gardens," in *In Search of Our Mothers' Gardens*, 231–43; her sense of activism, which is, for Walker, a reflection of her mother's ability to create beauty by establishing gardens in whatever neighborhood the family was in and her mother's connection to the earth as life giving, is recorded in the essay "The Only Reason You Want to Go to Heaven Is That You Have Been Driven Out of Your Mind (Off Your

of nature, and flowers in particular, that an ecowomanist lens gives special attention to this reference. It is more than an allusion to the diversity of colors among people. An ecowomanist perspective suggests that one must talk of how the diversity of colors of peoples is reflective of the diversity of types and colors of nature (in this case, flowers). It may seem obvious to some, however, that Walker's move to compare people to nature can be seen as a step toward developing the relationality between humans and nature. While neither the web-of-life concept nor any direct reference to African indigenous religious belief in the sacred connection between humans and the earth is made explicit in this part of the definition, Walker's comparison presents a foundational premise for ecowomanism: humans and nature are related to one another. This is illustrated in the diversity of humanity as mirrored in the diversity of nature.

Finally in part two, the ability of a womanist to survive and create pathways for surviving and thriving for others is referenced in the final fictive dialogue between a mother and daughter. This conversation describes the trek toward Canada (i.e., freedom from the oppressive treatment of blacks in the South). This final part of part two connotes hope-filled tones that resonate throughout the rest of the definition.

Part three of the *womanist* definition includes the most obvious reference to nature in that it points to a significant element of the earth—the moon. The presence of the moon as an element of nature is significant in itself, but what resonates more deeply with an ecowomanist perspective is the theoretical connection made between the moon and women. In religious traditions, including ancient forms of Christianity, goddess worship, Native American spiritualities, and African indigenous religions, a sacred connection is made between women and the moon. In *My Sister, My Brother: Womanist and Xodus God-Talk*, Karen Baker-Fletcher and Garth Fletcher refer to this reference to the moon, saying, "Walker emphasizes that

Land and Out of Your Lover's Arms): Clear Seeing Inherited Religion and Reclaiming the Pagan Self," in *Anything We Love Can Be Saved*, 3–27.

a womanist '*loves* the Spirit.' . . . This love is not separate . . . from love of nature and the cosmos (the moon). . . . Love of creation, Spirit, and Black women's culture are deeply intertwined and interrelated."[29]

The action-orientated word *love* is repeated eight times in the third part of the definition. This repetition highlights the strong theme of love captured throughout Walker's writings. Walker's concept of love expresses the importance of having emotional and relational ties to such things as music, dance, the moon, the Spirit, love, and food, as well as roundness, struggle, the folk, and herself regardless.[30] In addition to the attention given to the moon as an element of nature, it is also important to note the sequential order that Walker references loving the moon, and loving the Spirit.

Again here, as in part two of the definition, Walker infers a spiritual connection between nature and the spirit, which implies that there is a unique cosmological relationship between these two essences. From an ecowomanist perspective, the reference to food and roundness can also be connected to the earth as the giver or provider of food and the earth as the symbol of a circle or roundness. Understanding that a defining

---

[29] Fletcher and Fletcher, *My Sister, My Brother*, 5.

[30] It is important to note that the diverse ways that Walker *loves the Spirit* in the third part of the definition has been interpreted by womanist and nonwomanist scholars. A discussion engaging the meaning of this phrase and the appropriation of the term *womanist* is found in "Roundtable Discussion: Christian Ethics and Theology in Womanist Perspective," *Journal for Feminist Studies in Religion* 5 (1989): 83–112. The article began with a call-and-response format, with Cheryl J. Sanders articulating a challenge to womanist religious scholars to reexamine the appropriation of the term *womanist*. In her portion of the dialogical essay, Sanders critiqued the adoption of a *secular term* for the basis of Christian theological reflection and suggested that the lack of *God language* in the definition made use of the term problematic. I argue that "loves the Spirit" can have a variety of different meanings according to the womanist who is thinking through and appropriating the term that best fits her sense of spirituality and wholeness.

characteristic of Walker's activism arises from her understanding of love, it is appropriate that Walker's reference to loving struggle and loving the folk supports the premise that womanists are committed to the survival and wholeness of an entire people, explicated in part two.

Perhaps the most well-known part of the *womanist* definition is found at the end of part three, *loves herself regardless*. It is often highlighted as the central point in the *womanist* definition because it captures the spirit of womanism and its primary goals to empower and liberate women of African descent in their communities and the environment in which they live. Loving the self and accepting one's status as equal to any other human being points to the social and political aspects of the term in that Walker's emphasis on the sense of the self is clearly associated with the humanization of women. The value of humanization can be gleaned from Walker's recorded experiences of racism in the Deep South and during the civil rights movement. Similar to the way in which Walker suggests that racism fragments the self, society, history, and literature in essays like "The Civil Rights Movement: What Good Was It?"[31] her writings also suggest dehumanization occurs as an effect of racism. In her essay "Heaven Belongs to You: *Warrior Marks* as a Liberation Film," Walker uncovers the experiences of African American people who have endured generations of slavery and provides analysis of why humanization is a necessary value to hold in order to combat the dehumanizing impact racism has had on African American people.

> In my fifty years among African Americans I've noticed that, because of our suffering and our centuries-long insecurity, we have a hard time believing we are lovable. We also have a great fear of learning "bad" things about ourselves because we are sure these "bad" things will be cause for more people not to love us. . . . There is the

---

[31] Walker, "The Civil Rights Movement: What Good Was It?" in *In Search of Our Mothers' Gardens*, 119–29.

fear of being left behind, of being abandoned, of having no one on your side, if all your "stuff" is exposed. This feeling, which is very deep with us, is understandable: it is a legacy of our having been stolen from or expelled by Africa and rejected as human beings.[32]

By naming dehumanization as a part of the history of African Americans in the United States, Walker implies in her writings that humanization must become a value for African-descended people to practice and embody in resistance to oppressions.[33]

Finally, the fourth part of the definition, and also the short-est, simply and profoundly states, "Womanist is to feminist as purple is to lavender."[34] For womanist scholars this suggests that womanism brings forth a deeper color and deeper level of analysis than traditional feminist work, which looks primarily at gender. What makes gender-only analysis problematic is that it can disregard the interconnections between race, class, and gender that can have an impact on the way an African American woman, child, or man is treated in America. Having discussed the definition of *womanist*, coined by Walker as an important root of ecowomanism, as well as Walker's ecowomanist

---

[32] Walker, "Heaven Belongs to You: *Warrior Marks* as a Liberation Film," in *Anything We Love Can Be Saved*, 150.

[33] The value of humanization and, more specifically, self-humaniza-tion can also be gleaned from Walker's experience of watching her mother watch soap operas featuring white actors who played "Beautiful White People" on television in the 1950s. In the essay "The Civil Rights Move-ment: What Good Was It?" Walker critically reflects on the debilitating effects that embracing notions of white superiority can have on African peoples who are deceived into rejecting their own black skin. Describing her dismay after witnessing her mother's reaction to the television images of white beauty, wealth, and affluence, she infers that the values of self-love and self-humanization are necessary for African-descended women and African peoples to possess in order to resist modes of white suprem-acy and discard images that are constructed to make African peoples feel dehumanized.

[34] Walker, *In Search of Our Mothers' Gardens*, xi.

spirituality, let us turn toward the exploration of two additional models of ecowomanist spirituality in the work and scholarship of ecowomanist scholars Rose Mary Amenga-Etego and Mercy Oduyoye.

Rose Mary Amenga-Etego

The ecowomanist spirituality reflected in the lives, religion, and spirituality of Nankani women is deeply embedded in the culture and life of the community. Rose Mary Amenga-Etego's essay "Nankani Women's Spirituality and Ecology" is an invaluable resource to ecowomanist thought because it illustrates both Amenga-Etego's personal and communal religious commitments and practice of ecowomanist spirituality. As she writes, "Being a Nankani woman placed me in a unique position in this study. That is to say, not only did this study help to provide the needed insight and indigenous logical framework to some of the feminine beliefs and practices at the community level, it also enabled me as a researcher to acquire new knowledge ahead of time, in relation to the indigenous principles and practices."[35] Combining ethnographic methodology and religio-cultural approaches, the essay provides significant detail about Nankani culture and religion as well as opens the discourse of African spirituality, gender, religion, and ecology.

Amenga-Etego opens the essay by providing a definition of religion and ecology, and links these definitions to African spirituality. Citing her previous research in *Mending the Broken Pieces: Indigenous Religion and Sustainable Rural Development in Northern Ghana*,[36] the author highlights the

---

[35] Rose Mary Amenga-Etego, "Nankani Women's Spirituality and Ecology," *Worldviews: Global Religions, Culture, and Ecology* 20, no. 1 (2016): 16.

[36] Rose Mary Amenga-Etego, *Mending the Broken Pieces: Indigenous Religion and Sustainable Rural Development in Northern Ghana* (Trenton, NJ: Africa World Press, 2011).

uniqueness of the study of African religion. Building on the intellectual lineage of such African religion scholars as John S. Mbiti, Jacob Olupona, Kofi Asare Opoku, and others, she explains that African religion is not just a category about human life, but rather, as explained best by Opoku, is unique in that "traditional African religion [is] in its being a way of life."[37] Describing the important link between the spiritual and physical realms, as well as the interconnectedness between the spirit realm, natural realm, and human realm, the quote continues, "The purpose of religion is to order our relationship with our fellow-men and with our environment, both spiritual and physical. At the root of it is a quest for harmony between man, the spirit world, nature and society."[38] Having established the frame of interconnectedness, Amenga-Etego weaves four themes into the essay, including "the understanding of the environment as a sacred entity, its interconnectedness with life, and especially its place in African spirituality."[39] A fourth theme that she explicates addresses the second question raised in this chapter regarding the importance of spiritual activism in the lives of Nankani women. For the purpose of clarity, I will focus on the first three themes, and then explain the fourth in response to the second question.

The Environment as Sacred: The Earth as Sacred

The Nankani believe that the environment is sacred. Flowing from an African cosmology that connects the spirit realm, natural realm (earth), and the human realm, the belief in the sacredness of the environment promotes an ethical mandate to care for the earth. Amenga-Etego writes, "In many African communities, there is a strong belief that the spiritual is as much a part of the physical, as the physical is part of

---

[37] Amenga-Etego, "Nankani Women's Spirituality and Ecology," 17.

[38] Ibid.

[39] Ibid., 15.

all aspects of their daily lives. . . . This includes the natural environment."[40] As such, the guidance for life, or what we might call the ethical system of the community, is structured around the religio-cultural life of the community. This includes cultural rules and guidelines for communal interaction and relationships, as well as "rituals of pacification and restoration" that honor the "unseen natural order of the universe," including relationships with the creator (*Wine*), and between ancestral (*yan'duma*) and spirit entities (*baga*).

For Nankani, *Wine* is understood as the supreme creator and sustainer of the whole universe and the one who shapes the workings of life according to *paa'la* or destiny. *Paa'la* refers to direction, or *course of life*, and is used as a concept to help explain why and how things happen. That is, in the same vein that Christian-Judeo theological perspectives might understand *God's will*, *Wine* and *paa'la* are different from comparable concepts that help understand a human's role in caring for the earth, the role of the earth (nature) itself, and the creator's role in sustaining the earth and the whole universe, including the relationships between human beings, the earth, and the spirit realm.

The role of gender, and how it intersects with this interconnected reality, is the focus of Amenga-Etego's analysis. Referring to the unique relationships that Nankani women have with the calabash and other elements in nature because of their role as caretakers in the community, she writes that

---

[40] Ibid., 16. It is important to note that this sense of interconnectedness, as well as the understanding that the earth is sacred, is also shared as the first principle of the Environmental Justice People of Color Summit. The first principle quoted below is included in the list of principles, recorded in Dorceta E. Taylor, "The Rise of the Environmental Justice Paradigm: Injustice Framing and the Social Construction of Environmental Discourses," *American Behavioral Scientist* 43, no. 4 (2000): 566. It states, "Environmental justice affirms the sacredness of Mother Earth, ecological unity and the interdependence of all species, and the right to be free from ecological destruction."

"Nankani women's ecological views are dependent on [the] general understandings" of "Nankani spiritual notions and concerns in ecology."[41] From their roles as daughters, partners, wives, sisters, aunts, mothers, and sustainers of the community, it can be said that Nankani women share an identity with the earth as sustainers and providers of life for their community. This identity weaves together cultural, religious, and ecological or earth-keeping roles, since Nankani women are often responsible for gathering the elements of nature and sometimes perform rituals for the sake of their families. Amenga-Etego explains, "Invariably, they [Nankani women] view their roles of reproduction, nurturing and caring as an integral part of their destiny (paa'la) in this interconnected ecosystem."[42]

Gender and Interconnectedness of Ecosystem

> For most indigenous Nankani women, there is an acute knowledge of their special relationship with their environment. Until quite recently . . . women depended solely on their environment for all their needs. They made bowls, pots and water coolers from the soil. . . . As daughters, they are socialized to cut firewood, fetch water, harvest fresh vegetables and fruits. . . . In all these group activities, women are constantly engaged with nature.[43]

Noting the very important aspect of women's lives and women's work in Nankani culture, Amenga-Etego emphasizes how much of the work in women's lives is done communally and in deep connection with the environment. This connection between women and the environment is a strong and abiding theme in both ecowomanist and ecofeminist thought. The

---

[41] Amenga-Etego, "Nankani Women's Spirituality and Ecology," 25.
[42] Ibid.
[43] Ibid., 27.

latter is worth exploring here, since ecofeminist philosophy and ecofeminist spirituality have had an important influence on the shaping of ecowomanist thought. As I have explored in my previous research,[44] ecowomanist scholars Pamela Smith and Shamara Shantu Riley point this out best in their respective essays, "Green Lap, Brown Embrace, Blue Body: The Ecospirituality of Alice Walker," and "Ecology Is a Sistah's Issue Too: The Politics of Emergent Afrocentric EcoWomanism."[45]

In both works, the authors define *ecowomanism* in relation to ecofeminist thought, indicating that one theoretical foundation for ecowomanism is ecofeminist philosophy. In Smith's essay, she describes the term *ecowomanist*, saying, "Just as the term 'ecofeminist' expresses the perception that the degradation of the Earth [highlights] . . . the subordinating and bullying of women, racial, minorities, the poor, and the marginalized, the term 'ecowomanist' expresses the burden of this perception on a woman of color."

Similar to the way the term *womanist*, coined by Walker, was created to be "akin to feminist" but different, signaling the unique experiences of African American women and women of color's lives, ecowomanism also examines the particularities of women of color and African and African American women's perspectives on environmental justice.

Amenga-Etego also references the work of feminist scholars. Specifically she points to the work of Ursula King, whose observation of women's spirituality to be more fluid and not dualistic helps to undergird Amenga-Etego's explanation of African cosmology. King signals the importance of women's

---

[44] Melanie L. Harris, "Black Women, Religion and the Environment," *Black Scholar* 46, no. 3 (2016): 27–39.

[45] Pamela A. Smith, "Green Lap, Brown Embrace, Blue Body: The Ecospirituality of Alice Walker," *CrossCurrents* 48, no. 4 (1998/99): 471–87; Shamara Shantu Riley, "Ecology Is a Sistah's Issue Too," in *Liberating Faith: Religious Voices for Justice, Peace, and Ecological Wisdom*, ed. Roger E. Gottlieb, 412–27 (New York: Rowman & Littlefield, 2003).

spirituality for the discourse of feminism and describes spirituality as something that emerges out of "tensions, the fibres of our experience."

African Spirituality

While there are important differences between the terms *religion* and *spirituality* in Western religious discourse that heavily influence conversations in religion and ecology, Amenga-Etego's distinction between the two is also very important to acknowledge. Womanist scholar Layli Maparyan attempts to describe the former by saying, "Spirituality is not to be confused with religion. Religions exist to deliver people to a spiritual knowledge and its application. . . . For womanists, spirituality is an acknowledged relationship with the divine/transpersonal/cosmic/invisible realm, while religion is a culturally organized framework for experiencing that relationship."[46]

While Maparyan's definitions focus on the relationship with the *divine/transpersonal/cosmic/invisible realm* vs. a *culturally organized framework*, Amenga-Etego's observation helps to nuance the differences between the terms even more. She suggests that when we incorporate the discourse of ecology with reflections on African spirituality, a new question emerges about whether there is any difference between *spirituality* and *religion*. For her, there is reason to give pause and reflect on Jacob Olupona's question about why the word *spirituality* has recently gained so much currency.[47] This is an important point when reflecting on the frame of African cosmology that draws a connection between the various realms (divine/Spirit, nature/human) so that the study of religion also reflects this kind of interconnection and interdependence. As Amenga-Etego

---

[46] Maparyan, *The Womanist Idea*, 5.

[47] Jacob Olupona, "Sacred Ambiguity: Global African Spirituality, Religious Traditions, Social Capital and Self-Reliance," in *Global African Spirituality, Social Capital and Self-Reliance in Africa*, ed. Tunde Babawala and Akin Alao, xvii–xxxii (Lagos: Malthouse Press, 2008).

suggests, responses to the question "Where is the place of religion in matters of the environment?" will be different according to how one defines religion.

Spiritual Activism

For Amenga-Etego, just as African spirituality encompasses both personal and social aspects, so, too, is religion inclusive of the study to examine or reexamine the meaning and contextual understanding of belief, tradition, and culture. This understanding sheds light on Amenga-Etego's ecowomanist spirituality. Building on her extensive participant-observer research on Nankani women, she explains that while there are many "indigenous terms for the English term, 'religion,' the term *malba* best describes what the indigenous people perceive, believe and practice," that is, their ecowomanist spirituality.[48]

Mercy Oduyoye

Ecowomanist discourse is intentional in its inclusion of religious and ecowomanist spiritual perspectives across the diaspora. As such, the work of African feminist theologian Mercy Oduyoye is also significant in the work of ecowomanism.[49] Oduyoye's scholarship and especially her book *Introducing African Women's Theology*,[50] published in 2001, provides excellent sources for ecowomanism.

In her essay "The African Experience of God through the Eyes of an Akan Woman,"[51] Oduyoye describes the name

---

[48] Amenga-Etego, "Nankani Women's Spirituality and Ecology," 17.

[49] This section is a revised version of "Ecowomanism: Black Women, Religion, and the Environment," in *The Black Scholar* 46, no. 3 (2016): 27–39.

[50] Mercy Amba Oduyoye, *Introducing African Women's Theology* (Cleveland, OH: Pilgrim Press, 2001).

[51] Mercy Amba Oduyoye, "The African Experience of God through the Eyes of an Akan Woman," *CrossCurrents* 47, no. 4 (1997/98): 493–504.

of God as Nana, "the good parent, the grandparent" and explains that "some say he is father; others say she is mother. But the sentiment is the same; Nana is the source of loving-kindness and protection."[52] Nana is also depicted in some African religious traditions, such as Candomblé, as an orisha who is the beginning or creator of life. While African religions and theologies are diverse, and the religious perspectives of African women are even more varied, Oduyoye's description of the African woman's connection to the earth as an aspect of the divine parent is important for ecowomanist thought. In the essay she writes of the unity of God and the cosmos, saying, "God's sustenance and beneficence are seen in the rain as in the sunshine. . . . If there is too much rain or flood, we do not attribute them to God but to the anger of the divinities associated with nature or the ancestors whom we may have wronged by some unethical behavior or lack of reverence for what pertains to the spirit world. God always gives what is sufficient." Beyond her writings, Oduyoye's sharing of her own personal connection to the earth is an invaluable source for ecowomanism in that it adds a principle regarding the lifestyle and everyday actions embodied in an ecowomanist approach. In an interview that I conducted with the theologian in Gilford, Connecticut, on the occasion of her seventy-fourth birthday (October 21) on October 22, 2007, she spoke of her own understanding of her connection to nature, saying,

> I come from a very, very traditional family. We believe that there is a spiritual angle to everything that exists. . . . The material world, as we call it, is spiritual. And if you are not in tune with the material world then the likelihood is that you are not in tune with yourself and you are not in tune with your creator. So if I'm out walking (a daily practice), I feel like I'm part of nature. I may not be doing anything dramatic . . . but I feel

---

[52] Ibid., 495.

like part of nature. I love to garden and I feel myself, that if I have my hands in the soil, I feel like I'm centered. I try to have something living around me. . . . [Regarding animal life] I feel like . . . after all, these cats and dogs and so on they were all in the bush and we brought them, we domesticated them so we have a responsibility to make sure that they are ok, that's how I see it. And if I see a plant that is sitting there dying, I will say but how? Who planted this? Didn't they know that it needs water? I kind of empathize with things around me. So, in Ghana there is [an] emphasis on [the] green [belt] movement, and rebirth and so on. In my tradition when there is a flood, a river overflows, we always say the river is angry, the river is angry and when you look you will find that they have blocked the river someplace with rubbish that people have thrown in or something. So that's what I mean by, if nature is nice and beautiful—I feel ok. . . . I feel good when I'm in a place where nature looks good and is happy. . . . The empathy I have with creation is that they have a right to be here and they love life. If we have to take life in order to live, that's part of what the world is all about, but just destroying it is not allowed. . . . All life is life. If you have to survive by some of them, fine, but to destroy is not allowed—because we don't want our lives destroyed just for destruction's sake.

The daily walks that Oduyoye takes to spend devotional time with nature reveal the intimacy that she feels with nature. This idea is supported by a belief in African cosmology in which one's connection to nature is a reflection of one's connection with themselves and their creator. This form of devotion suggests another aspect of ecowomanism as a way of life and being in daily solidarity with the earth.

Ecowomanist Praxis:
Ecospirituality, Self-Care, and Earth Healing Practices

The religious lens of ecowomanism also points to earth-honoring faith practices led by women of African descent that provide models of contemplative practices of planetary and self-care. These kinds of ecospiritual healing practices help women connect the health of the self and community with the health of the planet. In other words, ecowomanism focuses on connections between black women's health, spiritualities, and ecological concerns. These connections are imperative to recognize, for as bell hooks suggests in her chapter "Touching the Earth," seeing the "correlation between the struggle for collective black self-recovery and the ecological movement . . . [propels us] to restore balance to the planet by changing our relationship to nature and to natural resources."[53] This moral call to engage in earth justice is one that has been echoed in the work of many social activist thinkers and social-prophetic voices in the black women's literary tradition, including Alice Walker, Emilie M. Townes, and Delores S. Williams. All of these women scholars highlight a moral imperative for earth justice, since this is embedded within the womanist notion of justice: access to wholeness and true flourishing for all living beings.

African American Environmental History and Healing Ecomemory

A return to hooks's claim that black self-recovery is connected to planetary recovery is helpful in setting additional context for ecowomanist and specifically African American environmental history. Whether through the work of the National Association for the Advancement of Colored People, encouraging people

---

[53] bell hooks, *Sisters of the Yam: Black Women and Self-Recovery* (New York: South End Press, 2005), 140.

to sign the Clean Air Act, or the herstory of Dorothy Height and the National Council of Negro Women, an organization that for decades has led initiatives in black and brown communities that focus on environmental health, contrary to the image presented by traditional environmental groups, the history of environmental action and justice work among African Americans is well documented.[54] Still, as a feminist theorist and cultural critic, hooks points out that there is a kind of mystical (if not spiritual) dignity and connection that African American peoples have shared with the land. Recognizing the spiritual, cultural, and historical significance of this connection helps scholars to recognize the African Americans' ecomemory and the shifts and changes in the agricultural knowledge that African Americans brought with them from the South to the North, for example, during the Great Migration.

Historians call the Great Migration one of the largest movements of human beings in history. It spanned six decades, from 1910 (some say 1915) to 1970, changing the lives of six million people, and is known to have set a new course for black life in American history. Influencing everything from urban planning and neighborhood development to regional cultural expressions, including those that gave birth to jazz music, the poetry of the Harlem Renaissance, and the prophetic call of the civil rights movement, the Great Migration is, in Isabel Wilkerson's words, "perhaps the biggest underreported story of the twentieth century."[55] Author of *The Warmth of Other Suns*, Wilkerson majestically weaves six decades of history through the amazing stories of three African Americans as they *tell the story* of their historic exodus from the South to the North.

As a source for ecowomanist reflection, hooks's book *Sisters of the Yam: Black Women and Self-Recovery* raises important questions as well as prompting responses and eco-

---

[54] Riley, 1993, 191–204.

[55] Isabel Wilkerson, *The Warmth of Other Suns: The Epic Story of America's Great Migration* (New York: Vintage, 2011), 9.

womanist reflection on African American or black women's literature. Diving into literary writings such as *Sula* by Toni Morrison[56] and *The Color Purple* by Alice Walker,[57] hooks shows how literary art is also a primary conversation partner in the work of black self-recovery and earth care. In the book, she raises examples within literature in which black women's experiences of joy and fullness, wholeness and health and love, are expressed through a poetic rendering of nature. Remarking on how important it is for black women's wholeness and health to consider the deep spiritual, emotional, and historical connection that black women, and black people, have with the earth, hooks notes that we are living in a time when we need to be reminded of our ecohistory, our connection with the earth—our ecomemory. She writes,

> Living in modern society, without a sense of history, it has been easy for folks to forget that black people were first and foremost a people of the land, farmers. It is easy for folks to forget that at the first part of the 20th century, the vast majority of black folks in the United States lived in the agrarian south. . . . There has been little to no work done on the psychological impact of the "Great Migration" of black people from the agrarian South to the industrialized North.[58]

hooks points out that the realities of loss, grief, and displacement may contribute to the psychological well-being and mental health of African American peoples living in the midst of environmentally hazardous communities today. Similar to the ways in which health providers, counselors, and pastoral care givers from a variety of faith communities today are helping African American communities deal with the posttraumatic stress of constant attacks on black lives, hooks signals that

---

[56] Toni Morrison, Sula (New York: Plume, 1981).

[57] Alice Walker, The Color Purple (New York: Harcourt, 1982).

[58] hooks, *Sisters of the Yam*, 137.

scholars need to pay attention to the healing practices that were and are being practiced daily to protect the psyches of black peoples. Some of those practices (also called spiritual care, self-care, or contemplative practices) engage the earth. For example, volunteers in the faith community of Friendship West Baptist Church in Dallas seasonally prepare the garden each year to plant okra, greens, tomatoes, and many other fresh fruits and vegetables. While not directly named a contemplative practice of healing, historically gardening in black life is known as a healing practice that can reduce stress, embolden agency, and build community.[59] Other models of community gardens can be found across the country, from faith communities in Chicago to rooftops in New York. When we consider how the practice of gardening, planting, and reconnecting to the earth can have positive neurological and psychological impacts, then we, as scholars and activists, are moved to open up the discourse to an ecowomanist reality of honoring the connection with the earth as healing.

The connection between African American and Native American history that hooks mentions in her book is also important to expand upon because of the healing practices that it offers for communities of color engaged in environmental justice or ecojustice movements. Noting the depths of loss and feelings of ecological grief and displacement that accompany the lives and stories of many peoples of Native ancestry, Native literary poet Beata Tsosie Peña directly addresses ecological loss and violence, claiming that hope remains and can be ignited through the practice of social justice activism. For example, in the work of TEWA Women's United, one can find evidence of community empowerment and attention to ecological justice as well as women's liberation.[60] These examples of how to create healing practices and also uncover practices

---

[59] Vaughn Sills, *Places for the Spirit: The Tradition of African American Gardens* (San Antonio, TX: Trinity University Press, 2010).

[60] Beata Tsosie Peña, "Mother's Moment," November 13, 2012, https://www.youtube.com/watch?v=_rnOtysdulo.

within Native, indigenous, and African American earth-honoring faith traditions is a part of the work of ecowomanism. As I have outlined above, the approach begins with a methodological step of acknowledging and uncovering African American peoples' ecomemory and connection with the earth. As a practical step, it also moves to recall the "legacy of our ancestors who knew that the way we regard the land and nature will determine the level of our self-regard"[61] and helps African and African American communities claim their healing connection with the earth.

---

[61] hooks, *Sisters of the Yam*, 140.

CHAPTER FIVE

Ecowomanist Interreligious Dialogue

To be a womanist is to be inherently interfaith.[1] The contours and depth of the definition and dialogue about the various theological perspectives, historical and life experiences, religious beliefs, and ethical mores of women of African descent necessitate an interfaith mode of engagement. Black women and their belief systems are not monolithic. Contrary to the fantastic hegemonic imagination and other essentialist myths, African, African American, and/or black women's identities and religious identities are sacredly diverse.[2] According to third-wave womanist approaches that include attention to interdisciplinary methods; analysis of intersections between gender, globalization, and peacebuilding; and an interreligious landscape, women of African descent embody a variety of religiosities, ethical worldviews,

---

[1] This chapter is a revised version of my earlier essay, "Womanist Interfaith Dialogue: Inter, Intra, and All the Spaces in Between," in *Postcolonial Practice of Ministry: Leadership, Liturgy, and Interfaith Engagement*, ed. Kwok Pui-lan and Stephen Burns, 199–214 (New York: Lexington Books, 2016).

[2] Emilie M. Townes, *Womanist Ethics and the Cultural Production of Evil* (New York: Palgrave Macmillan, 2006).

and political ideologies that create a beautiful array of complex subjectivity and ways of living in community with the earth.[3]

One word that describes the sense of agency and choice that womanists have in self-naming and embracing their religious identity or spirituality is *lifesystem*. This term is explained best by Layli Maparyan and is inclusive of a variety of religious, indigenous, and faith traditions, as well as mystical and metaphysical belief systems. She writes that the use of the term helps to distinguish religion from spirituality, an important distinction to make for womanist religious thought in that one refers to a culturally organized framework (religion) and the other acknowledges relationship with the divine realm (spirituality). Maparyan explains that both are important: "Historically, religion has been the province of institutionalized structures, while spirituality as such has been the province of mysticism and metaphysics. Yet the two are connected and interpenetrating in ways that, again, require new language."[4] The new term, *lifesystem*, is important in that it offers a model of womanist ingenuity and agency to produce "new language that fits us" in the same way and in the same spirit that Alice Walker coined the term *womanist* separate and apart from *feminist*, and in the way that Katie G. Cannon, Delores S. Williams, and other womanist scholars have created new language to explain the multivocal nature of black women's religiosities and theological perspectives.[5] Lifesystem is also innovative and in keeping with third-wave womanist perspectives; it reaches "beyond womanism,"[6] past the use of

---

[3] Melanie L. Harris, *Gifts of Virtue, Alice Walker, and Womanist Ethics* (New York: Palgrave Macmillan, 2010).

[4] Harris, "Womanist Interfaith Dialogue: Inter, Intra, and All the Spaces in Between," 200.

[5] See Walker's explanation of why and how the term *womanist* was distinct from feminism in her essay "Audre's Voice," in *Anything We Love Can Be Saved: A Writer's Activism* (New York: Random House, 1997), 80.

[6] Karla Simcikova, *To Live Fully, Here and Now: The Healing Vision in the Works of Alice Walker* (New York: Lexington Books, 2007).

traditional religious Christian-centered theological categories used in the discourse, and provides a term that "allows Hinduism, Judaism, Zoroastrianism, Buddhism, Christianity, Islam, the Baha'i faith, and all other 'institutionalized' religions to be on equal footing with African traditional and African-derived religions, Native American religious traditions, Aboriginal religious traditions, and all other 'indigenous' spiritual systems."[7] This equal footing that Maparyan suggests opens up the dialogue of womanist religious thought to be more inclusive of new language and new categories necessary for interfaith and interreligious dialogue.

Like Walker's creative and scholarly development of the new word *womanist* in the late 1970s, Maparyan's introduction of the term *lifesystems* to womanist discourse helps point to the positive nature of difference expressed in the definition of *womanist*. Just as there are diverse embodiments of color recognized in the various shades and skin tones of women in womanist communities, so, too, are the religious lives of women of African descent throughout the diaspora varied and beautiful with "every color represented."[8] When we examine more closely the definition of womanist by Walker, we find "more room in it for changes"[9] and an openness to religious spiritual practices and interpretations of *Spirit*, since this is defined as an important aspect of a womanist life and perspective.[10] Womanist religious thought also gives celebratory and positive attention to the various particularities of religion and religious life practiced by women of African descent. Recognized as a theory and praxis, womanist religious thought

---

[7] Layli Maparyan, *The Womanist Idea* (New York: Routledge, 2012), 5.

[8] Alice Walker, "Womanist," in *In Search of Our Mothers' Gardens: Womanist Prose* (New York: Harcourt Brace and Jovanovich, 1983).

[9] Walker, "Audre's Voice," 79–82.

[10] Womanist scholar Layli Maparyan argues in her work *The Womanist Idea* that this connection to Spirit in its various manifestations is one of the aspects of womanism that makes it unique and different from traditional black feminism. See Maparyan, *The Womanist Idea*.

examines the plethora of religious ideas, practices, ethical ideals, sacred texts, and more that shape the religious perspectives and spiritual practices of women of African descent.

Womanist Roots

Womanism emerged out of a (mostly) North American context focusing on the lives of African Americans and later reached out to the wider African diaspora. In intellectual circles and academic and activist realms, scholars and thinkers began adopting Walker's term *womanist* as a descriptor of the socioanalytical method used to highlight the complex subjectivity of black women. Their use of race–class–gender analysis in the social movements of the 1960s placed attention on the importance of civil rights, gender, and economic equality for black women. In these social movement settings, womanism emerged out of dialogue with those in the *mainstream* (read: white) feminist movement who exposed sexism and the unfair advantage of men over women in the United States and globally. These feminists (often white) pointed out gender disparities in everything from access to education, job salary equity, women's bodily rights, and health care, but they regularly neglected race as a category to examine when looking at these same issues and their impact on women of color.

Regarding civil rights, many African American women leaders and activists participated deeply in the struggle for the rights of African Americans and other peoples of color to have the right to vote and for the dismantling of the Jim and Jane Crow system, an oppressive system that legalized brutal acts of racial violence such as lynchings and segregation. A focus on gender and race, as well as economic justice, framed a *tripartite* analytical frame that guided activists, leaders, teachers, and everyday black women and men to push for political social action, policy change, and equal rights. This kind of race–class–gender analytical frame became a foundational theoretical base for womanist and (later) feminist thinkers.[11]

---

[11] For more on the engagement with race in early feminist thought, see

Womanism Is Postcolonial

It is important to note that womanism emerged out of an insistence that this kind of tripartite focus be taken seriously in *all* social justice action and interrogation of theoretical development. This methodological move to use race–class–gender analysis as an embedded part of a womanist lens is also a postcolonial move. In sync with an impulse to self-define even in the midst of a colonial myth about the self or community, womanist analysis is postcolonial because it insists that a lens be developed and used that *demystifies* inaccurate cultural representations of black women that are designed to rob women themselves of power and agency. Breaking from traditional Eurocentric lenses that historically view black women as victims lacking in moral character and self-respect, womanist analysis pushes beyond notions of Western aesthetics. Instead, the focus is on the beauty and complexity of black women's lives and the depth of sheer wisdom that comes from black women who daily navigate and survive shifting oppressive systems. Naming structural racism, classism, and sexism as oppressive systems, womanism exposes the underside of colonialism and its impact historically on the lives of black women as well as the lack of access to opportunity they have experienced. The field of womanist ethics particularly reflects postcolonial theory and practice in that it mines the moral systems and ethical values of black women by validating women's voices, experience, and story as valid epistemology. Shifting the power of the production of knowledge, womanist religious thought (and especially womanist ethics) critiques traditional Western logic, wherein black women are rarely considered fully human. It problematizes the use of hierarchal value dualisms. Finally, rather than using a sole category of analysis through which to examine black women's lives, theological

---

the works of bell hooks, *Feminism Is for Everybody: Passionate Politics* (Cambridge, MA: South End Press, 2000), and Melanie L. Harris, "Womanist Humanism: A Deeper Look," *CrossCurrents* 57, no. 3 (2007): 391–403.

interpretations, or religious ideas, womanist analysis necessitates a combination of lenses be used to rehumanize black women in a logic of domination, and circumvents that logic by placing epistemological privilege on black women's voices, stories, and experiences. This connection between theory and praxis in womanist religious thought is key in both the intellectual development of womanist thought and in womanist activism.

Within activist circles in the civil rights movement, figures like Fannie Lou Hamer, Ella Baker, and Diane Nash arose as some of the most prominent voices that consistently pointed out the connections between gender, economics, and racial disenfranchisement.[12] In the feminist movement, other voices emerged, including bell hooks, Audre Lorde, and Alice Walker; each pointed out the flaws in feminist thinking to attempt to universalize all women's justice concerns according to a paradigm based on the life experience of middle- to upper-class white women. As formative leaders and thinkers, hooks, Lorde, and Walker's very embodiment as racial, gendered, and sexual selves fighting for economic justice and gender and racial equality was itself a message to and from the movement. There was often a disconnect between white women involved in the early feminist movement and black, Latina, Asian, and Native American women who refused to lay down their racial identity or their communities to *fit* within white feminism.

hooks writes explicitly about these tensions within the feminist movement in the early years:

> They [white women] entered the movement erasing and denying difference, not playing race alongside gender, but eliminating race from the picture. Foregrounding gender meant that white women could take center stage, could claim the movement as theirs, even as they called on all women to join. The utopian vision of sisterhood evoked

---

[12] See Rosetta Ross, *Witnessing and Testifying: Black Women, Religion, and Civil Rights* (Minneapolis: Fortress Press, 2003).

in a feminist movement that initially did not take racial difference or anti-racist struggle seriously did not capture the imagination of most black women/women of color.[13]

Pushing the boundaries of the feminist movement to be inclusive of race, two primary discourses grew out of this struggle: black feminism and womanism. The term *womanist* was coined by Walker to distinguish the complex subjectivity of black women and to help explain why their insistence of the acceptance of their *whole* selves (racial, economic, gender, sexual identities, and more) was imperative to acknowledge if true social justice was to be achieved. She coined the term in the late 1970s in an essay entitled "Coming Apart," later providing the four-part definition discussed above in her nonfiction collection of essays *In Search of Our Mothers' Gardens: Womanist Prose*. In later conversation with Lorde and others, Walker expanded the meaning of the term to be inclusive of women's sexuality and political ideology.[14]

Home: Womanist Epistemology and Interfaith Womanist Dialogue

Scholars and religious leaders working in the discipline of religion also adopted the term *womanist*. Katie Cannon's landmark essay "The Emergence of Black Feminist Consciousness" ignited a firestorm in the world of theology and ethics.[15] Suddenly, marginalized voices of African American women were shifting themselves to the center and arguing that the entire discourse of theology was incomplete without hearing the

---

[13] hooks, *Feminism Is for Everybody*, 56.

[14] See Walker, "Audre's Voice," 79–82. Also see Alice Walker's "Democratic Womanism: A Poem" (October 2012), http://alicewalkersgarden.com/2012/10/article-i-will-not-vote-for-evil-i-want-a-different-system/.

[15] Katie G. Cannon, "The Emergence of Black Feminist Consciousness," in *Katie's Cannon: Womanism and the Soul of the Black Community* (New York: Continuum, 1998), 47–56.

voices of women, and women of African descent. Arguments
from every angle began to take shape for the emergence of
womanist religious thought. There were those who, like Cannon, provided black feminist methodology as a base from
which to grow womanist *gardens* and praxis and scholarship.
There were also scholars who rooted the heart of womanism
in black women's interpretation of the Bible (Renita Weems)
and still others who argued that different theological categories were necessary to examine if in fact black women's voices
were to be heard in Christian theology (Delores S. Williams
and Jacquelyn Grant). Responding "yes" to the invitation to
engage theology from the heart of their own womanist identity, these women adopted the term *womanist* from Walker,
giving special attention to the phrase in the definition, a womanist "Loves the *Spirit*."[16]

In *Gifts of Virtue, Alice Walker, and Womanist Ethics*, I
argued that the term *womanist* and its acknowledgment of
Spirit opened wide the door for theological and religious
inquiry for all those who chose to be womanist. That is, even
as the term was often problematized and questioned, it was
indeed adopted by several womanist religious scholars in
the 1980s. Some from a more evangelical branch of Christianity argued that the inclusion of the reference to *Spirit* in
the definition was not *Christian* enough and did not point
toward Christian roots or origins. There was deep concern
expressed by Cheryl Sanders that the definition of *womanist*
was inclusive of lesbian, gay, bisexual, and transgender persons; and for her, this was not in keeping with the community
of Christ.[17] Still other scholars in these first-wave womanist
debates argued that, methodologically, the term fits the larger
goals and scholarly direction in which womanist theology and
ethics were moving.

---

[16] Walker, *In Search of Our Mothers' Gardens*.

[17] Cheryl J. Sanders, "Roundtable Discussion: Christian Ethics and
Theology in Womanist Perspective," *Journal for Feminist Studies in Religion* 5 (1989): 83–112.

The Womanist Dancing Mind, Method, and Interfaith Womanist Dialogue

As first-wave debates opened the door for new discourse in the second and third waves of womanist scholarship, scholars such as Emilie M. Townes began to develop important methods to uncover and understand African life and religion. In regard to interfaith dialogue, Townes offers an exceptional method that opens and expands the discourse. There is a remarkable religious plurality alive in the African diaspora that speaks to the richness of African tradition and heritage. As a religious scholar and womanist ethicist with a scholarly eye toward justice and hope, she points to the value of this heritage as womanist and African American epistemology, and argues that a specialized approach with attention to the vastness of the particular be used when studying the interreligious contours of womanist religious and African American religious thought.[18]

Shaping a method to do this kind of work, Townes moves away from modes of destructive criticism (similar to those in most literary and academic discourses) and moves toward constructive criticism. Making a classic womanist methodological turn,[19] she chooses African American women's literature to shed light on the construction of a womanist scholarly method. She cites the work of Toni Morrison and the dancing mind: "There is a certain kind of peace that is not merely the absence of war. . . . The peace I am thinking of is the dance of an open mind when it engages another equally open one—an activity that occurs most naturally, most often in the reading/writing world we live in."[20]

---

[18] Townes, *Womanist Ethics and the Cultural Production of Evil.*

[19] See my analysis of Katie G. Cannon's methodological step to incorporate African American and African American women's literature as a primary source for womanist thought in Melanie L. Harris, "A Path Set before Us: Womanist Virtue Method," in *Gifts of Virtue*, 49–59.

[20] Toni Morrison, *The Dancing Mind* (New York: Alfred A. Knopf, 1996), 7–8.

Morrison's concept of the dancing mind can be summarized as the creation and tending to of an embodied space of peace in which minds meet and dance in openness with one another. Absent of harsh criticism and judgment so often associated with religious dialogue, in which one tradition is attempting to convert the other, the dancing mind is a kind of mutually enhancing engagement of thought. Creatively writing in a style that is reflective of this kind of mutuality, Townes responds to Morrison's idea:

> It is in the dancing mind that many of us meet each other more often than not. . . . It is in this dancing mind— where we tease through the possibilities and the realities, the hopes, the dreams, the nightmares, the terrors, the critique, the analysis, the plea, the witness—that womanist work is done in the academy, in the classroom, in the religious gatherings of our various communities, in those quiet and not so quiet times in which we try to reflect on the ways in which we know and see and feel and do. . . . This womanist dancing mind is one that comes from a particular community of communities yearning for a common fire banked by the billows of justice and hope. As such, this particularity marks us with indelible ink. My task is to explore the twists and turns of the communities from which we spring and have our very life and breath. It is to be particular about the particular—and explore the vastness of it.[21]

The "vastness" of the particular that Townes is addressing here is both the geographical and religious plurality alive in the communal religious practices and people of the African diaspora. In this sense, Townes's concept of the womanist dancing mind is both art and a method of doing interre-

---

[21] Townes, *Womanist Ethics and the Cultural Production of Evil*, 1–2.

ligious and interfaith work that looks at the "assortments of African American life" and beyond. Here, she describes how the womanist method is being used in an interreligious context:

> The womanist dancing mind—the one what weaves in and out of Africa, the Caribbean, Brazil, the United States (South, North, East and West); the Christian, the Jewish, the Muslim, the Candomblé, the Santeria, the Vodun, the Native American, the casts of color, the sexuality, the sexual orientation, the socioeconomic class, the age, the body image, the environment, the pedagogies, the academy—has before it an enormous communal task. One in which we are trying to understand the assortments of African American life. If I do this task well, I will realize the ways in which Black life is not my life alone, but a compendium of conscious and unconscious coalitions with others whose lives are not lived solely in the Black face of United States life. . . . I am interested in exploring the depths of African American life—female and male. For it is in exploring these depths, in taking seriously my particularity—not as a form of essentialism, but as epistemology—where I can meet and greet others for we are intricately and intimately interwoven in our postmodern culture.[22]

The method of the womanist dancing mind recognizes the complexities of a globalized world in the lives of women of African descent and highlights the importance of interdisciplinary (religio–social–literary) approaches. It especially signals that fresh attention should be made to the interreligious nature of African, African American, and black religious life. Furthermore, the method is undergirded with an

---

[22] Ibid., 2.

ethical frame reflective of its connection with the history of black intellectual thought where life itself sparks a fire in the hearts of those committed to uncovering the retentions of African life and moral and religious principles such as peace, harmony with the earth, and justice; these are all aims of interfaith dialogue.

Townes's method of the womanist dancing mind is hopeful and useful in determining the best ways to promote interfaith dialogue and recognize the importance of interreligious realities in the heart of womanist religious thought.[23] There is something beautiful about the religious plurality housed within womanist epistemologies that simultaneously honors and embodies interreligious and, in some cases, intrareligious dialogue and practice.[24]

---

[23] And even more specifically in the heart of womanist spirituality that is interreligious by nature, which helps to shape a method for peacebuilding and social and earth justice.

[24] I have found Raimon Panikkar's understanding and interpretation of intrareligious dialogue most helpful in explaining the experience that many African American women have as they explore religious practices that are healing for their self-esteems and value systems, which are sometimes outside of the faith traditions that they were born into. See Raimon Panikkar, *The Rhythm of Being—The Unbroken Trinity: The Gifford Lectures* (Maryknoll, NY: Orbis Books, 2013). For more discussion on these realities, see my discussion of fluid and hybrid womanist spiritualities in *Gifts of Virtue*, where I write, "One of the hallmarks of third-wave womanism is to be more inclusive of various religious perspectives held by women of African descent across the Diaspora . . . and I argue that Townes' work is a model out of which third-wave womanist approaches find grounding. . . . Building upon Townes' work, third-wave womanist approaches examine the ways in which many women of African descent combine aspects of a variety of religions to shape a spiritual path that empowers them to overcome oppressions" (ibid., 136). Also see Melanie L. Harris, "Buddhist Resources of Womanist Reflection," *Journal of Buddhist-Christian Studies* 34 (2014): 107–14.

Eyes toward Justice:
The Value of Interdisciplinary Approaches and Global Links in Womanist Interfaith Dialogue

The emphasis on justice in womanist religious thought and the accompanying political nature of womanist interfaith dialogue cannot be overlooked. I now turn to some of the other important sociological and politically based social justice discourses that play a role in the establishment of interfaith womanism.

Postmodern approaches in womanist religious thought will point to the importance of teaching the varieties of religion alive in communities of African peoples for many reasons. One of the most important is the emphasis on the history of African peoples to survive and find a quality of life, especially in the North American context where the will to live was tested daily. Religion served as a tool for hope, meaning making, and survival for enslaved African peoples forced to breed, provide free labor, and build the economic base for the United States.

Taking a historical look beyond the discourse that illuminates the rich history and practice of African indigenous religious traditions, Egyptian Coptic Christianity, and the history of Islam on the continent of Africa, the debates between sociologists Melville Jean Herskovits and E. Franklin Frazier provide an important and interdisciplinary entry into the dialogue of interfaith womanism. First published in 1941, Herskovits's landmark book, *The Myth of the Negro Past*, argued against accepted claims of the time (such as Frazier's) that offered a negative portrayal of Africa.[25] This shift was exemplified in the writings of eighteenth-century poet and pioneering African American woman writer Phillis Wheatley. Rejecting the enforced shame and denial of Africa, Herskovits disagreed with arguments that the Middle Passage and enslavement of African peoples permanently damaged any cultural memory

---

[25] Melville J. Herskovits, *The Myth of the Negro Past* (New York: Harper, 1941).

that Africans had linking them to their past heritage. Instead, he argued that there were many cultural retentions (Africanisms) that survived the traumatic journey and history of African Americans. Herskovits's scholarship laid the groundwork for later African American literary and religious scholars, such as Zora Neale Hurston, and contemporary scholars, such as Donald Matthews, to investigate the retention of African storytelling rites and religious rituals that make obvious the connection between African American religious communities and a host of other African communities across the diaspora.[26] The uncovering of Africanisms, especially through the practice of religion, can be described as a multiple-edged sword in that it cut through the myths and dynamic movement of the fantastic hegemonic imagination. That is, with this truth regarding African peoples' connection and cultural remnants, not only could a link to African culture be restored, but also a recognition of the explosion of African retentions (religious and cultural) that spread like fire, even as the horrific and violent act of the transatlantic slave trade was taking place. Interreligious, intrareligious, and interfaith African American and, specifically, womanist religious thought (global in its approach) are examples of this cultural and historical explosion.

Although she is often overlooked, anthropologist Zora Neale Hurston is a very scholarly source for the argument for religious plurality within the African diasporic context. By centering African and African American peoples' religious history and political demand for rights, Hurston's research on the retentions of African rites and rituals, and Caribbean religious expression and culture, suggested that black religious lives matter and are a crucial part of the project of understanding religion. In addition to writing about voodoo and hoodoo in the deep southern United States, Hurston's work also took a kind of interfaith turn as she researched the religious lives of women and their communities in Haiti and Jamaica. As such,

---

[26] Donald Matthews, *Honoring the Ancestors: An African Cultural Interpretation of Black Religion* (New York: Oxford University Press, 1998).

her work also paves a path for contemporary religious scholars to take up the proven existence of religious plurality and global links in African diasporic and especially African American religious life.[27] This reality of religious plurality, in the context of mainstream scholarly pluralist (versus exclusivist or inclusivist) approaches to religion, suggests that interfaith dialogue is not only a part of womanist religious thought, but a foundation of the discourse.

Interfaith, Interreligious, and Intrareligious Womanism

Interfaith and interreligious womanism acknowledges a rich diversity of religious orientations, lifesystems, and spiritualities practiced by women of African descent and others who identify as womanist and apply womanist teachings and approaches to their justice work. In keeping with the three hallmarks of third-wave womanist approaches that I have articulated in my previous work,[28] interfaith womanism (1) explores the interreligious landscape of African diasporic perspectives through the use of comparative religious and interfaith approaches, (2) uses interdisciplinary methods and approaches to find strategies of justice keeping and peacebuilding,[29] and (3) examines the impact of globalization and links across the African diaspora. In part, these hallmarks help to focus a path toward uncovering similar and distinct ethical imperatives for justice in a variety of religious traditions and spiritual practices. For the sake of clarity, this section will describe the distinctions between interfaith, interreligious, and intrareligious from a womanist perspective.

---

[27] Zora Neale Hurston, *Tell My Horse: Voodoo and Life in Haiti and Jamaica* (New York: J. P. Lippincott, 1938). Also see Zora Neale Hurston, *Mules and Men* (New York: J. P. Lippincott, 1935).

[28] Melanie L. Harris, "Third-Wave Womanism: Expanding Womanist Discourse, Making Room for Our Children," in *Gifts of Virtue*, 125–38.

[29] Ibid.

Interfaith Womanist Dialogue

Delores S. Williams, a founding mother in womanist theology, explains the heart of womanism and the purpose of the discourse best in her book *Sisters in the Wilderness: The Challenge of Womanist God-Talk*.[30] She states, "Womanist theology especially concerns itself with the faith, survival and freedom-struggle of African-American women," and explains why it is so important to express the particularity of African American women's faith perspectives, theologies, and religious worldviews. The reason for this is in part because these perspectives are too often overlooked or underappreciated by normative religious discourse. While maintaining a liberationist frame that "challenges all oppressive forces impeding black women's struggle for survival and for the development of a positive, productive quality of life conducive to women's and the family's freedom and well-being . . . (and) opposes all oppression based on race, sex, class, sexual preference, physical disability and caste," Williams insists that womanist theology goes even further than this.[31]

Perhaps one of the most inspiring aspects of Williams's articulation of womanist theology (within the first wave of womanist theology) is its insistence on transformation through dialogue. An important step in Williams's method and her understanding of womanism opens the door for interfaith dialogue and collaboration. While Williams grounds her own perspective of womanist theology from the lens of Christian liberation theology, I argue that her words can be interpreted to encourage us to open the door of womanist discourse beyond this perspective. Regarding the importance of dialogue, she writes,

---

[30] Delores S. Williams, *Sisters in the Wilderness: The Challenge of Womanist God-Talk* (Maryknoll, NY: Orbis Books, 1993), xiv–xv.

[31] One might note the similar tone and broad reach of Williams's articulation here and bell hooks's often-quoted and inclusive definition of feminism: "Feminism is a movement to end sexism, sexist exploitation, and oppression," in *Feminism Is for Everybody*, xiii.

Womanist theology is usually non-separatist and dialogical. It welcomes discourse with a variety of theological voices—liberation, white feminist, Mujerista,
Jewish, Asian, African, classical and contemporary
"male-stream," as well as non-feminist, non-womanist
female voices. Womanist theology considers one of its
primary tasks to dialogue with the church and with
other disciplines.[32]

Taking this challenge seriously and building it alongside the
hallmarks of third-wave womanists, we see a frame for interfaith womanist dialogue.

The term and reflective practice of interfaith dialogue
began after Vatican II. While many scholars argue that religious faiths certainly had encounters with each other centuries before, Vatican II greatly shifted the theological orientation to non-Christians. Instead of holding missionizing and
evangelizing approaches as the sole ways to engage persons
of various religious orientations, Vatican II promoted reflection on the sacred truths in various religions. Documenting
this history, Kwok Pui-lan describes interfaith dialogue as
"sustained reflection on dialogue and religious plurality."[33]
The discourse widens the door for people of different faiths
to creatively and critically engage each other's faiths and supports them "working together to address shared problems of
a local community or wider concerns."[34] Since social justice
issues and the impact of globalization are key hallmarks to
third-wave womanism, this understanding of interfaith fits
well with the practice of interfaith communities in womanist
communities.

---

[32] Ibid., xiv–xv.

[33] Kwok Pui-lan, *Globalization, Gender and Peacebuilding: The
Future of Interfaith Dialogue* (New York: Paulist Press, 2012), 22.

[34] Ibid.

Interreligious Womanist Dialogue

The emphasis on dialogue mentioned in Williams's method and understanding of womanist theology is also a key factor in interreligious womanist dialogue. Often used interchangeably, in fact, interreligious conversations can have a different starting point than interfaith dialogue. The former often dives into the depth of difference between doctrine, dogma, and theology, but can also give attention to reflection on religious experiences from a different tradition and faith encounters, wherein one's own *home* faith is deepened or reflected on differently as a result of sustained critical engagement with another faith tradition.[35] For womanist religious thought, interreligious dialogue might also take on another dimension whereby practitioners share an ethical worldview such as the moral imperative for earth justice that arises from a shared African cosmological outlook that connects divine, nature, and human realms.[36] As previously discussed, shared racial, ethnic, or cultural identity that peoples of African descent share across the diaspora can also have an impact on interreligious dialogue. There is often a link between people's experiences of having to defend their own humanity in a context that is controlled by white supremacy. Whether these experiences of survival emerge from persons of African descent enduring racism in America or surviving British or European colonialism, the experiences and religious reflection on them can serve as an important link that connects these peoples who may practice and be guided by different religious worldviews.[37]

[35] See the work of Paul F. Knitter, *Without Buddha I Could Not Be a Christian* (Oxford: Oneworld Press, 2009).

[36] See Melanie L. Harris, "An Ecowomanist Vision," in *Ethics That Matters: African, Caribbean and African American Sources*, ed. James Logan and Marcia Y. Riggs, 189–93 (Minneapolis: Fortress Press, 2012).

[37] Of course these points of similarities can also operate as points of difference. Just as Kwok Pui-lan's book *Globalization, Gender and Peacebuilding* points out, it is important to note the multiple layers of privileg

Depending on the setting, these connections can at times transcend religious differences for the sake of thinking together and finding answers to global social problems. One example of this is a gathering I attended in Ghana, West Africa, in July 2012. The "African and African Diasporan Women in Religion and Theology Conference" was hosted by African feminist theologian Mercy Oduyoye at Trinity Theological Seminary's Talitha Qumi Institute of African Women in Religion and Culture in Legon, Ghana. The focus of the conference was finding practical solutions, theological sources, and methods that would help end violence against women and girls of African descent. Participants came from various African cultures and religious traditions, including Islam, Christianity, and several African indigenous religions. In large and small group discussions, there was a genuine sense of interfaith community developed in part because the emphasis was finding a solution to an ethical problem. At one point, I recall a woman leader and teacher in Islam having a conversation with a Christian participant who posed a question about the value of women's bodies in religion. What unfolded was an extraordinary exchange about interpretations of the story of Esther as told in narratives and sacred stories from Islam and how these truths might open up Christian readings of Esther. While this discussion did not involve critical comparison of language, source of literature, and doctrinal differences, the interreligious dialogue that occurred was central to sharing religious viewpoints of how to create and sometimes rediscover woman-affirming narratives from religious texts and interreligious dialogue.

—religious, economic, and otherwise (Western, capitalistic, colorism, or internalized sexism or racism, etc.)—that can also work against mutual sharing and trust necessary for interreligious dialogue. Being aware of these points of privilege and forming a method that immediately attends to these in an effort to create honest mutuality is very important for successful interreligious dialogue.

Intrareligious Womanist Dialogue

As more and more millennials describe themselves as *spiritual but not religious*, scholars, religious practitioners, and faith leaders have begun to ask questions regarding the context in which this generation has learned about religion. Globalization, quick and easy access to information about sacred truths held by people and religious communities all over the planet, and a rise in an interest that many millennials have in social action are some of the factors that scholars believe influence their decisions about religious identity.

At the same time, it has also been observed that millennials, as well as many in older generations, see the world of religion as a cornucopia of choices and religion itself as a place of agency and self-naming. That is, many find that their own choice to be or identify as religious or not, embrace multiple religious belongings, or to become intrareligious are all agency-producing choices. From a womanist perspective, this is not surprising. Considering the impact that the history of the black church and African American religious life has had and the agency-inspiring empowerment of African and African American communities (from the civil rights movement to the movement to eradicate mass incarceration),[38] there is more acceptance of the right to choose one's religion and practice spirituality in these communities than one might think.

Intrareligious womanist spirituality examines ways in which many women of African descent combine aspects of a variety of religions to shape a spiritual path that empowers them to overcome oppressions, name themselves, and create wholeness for their own lives and imagine wholeness for the whole earth community. Similar to the articulation of intrareligious dialogue by Panikkar, this form of religious practice relies heavily on self-reflection regarding various religious experiences, theological shifts, and transformations that occur

---

[38] See Michelle Alexander, *The New Jim Crow: Mass Incarceration in the Age of Colorblindness* (New York: New Press, 2010).

as a result of encountering more than one religion simultaneously. The *inner dialogue* that occurs in intrareligious reflection can be seen as another aspect of the womanist directive: dialogue.[39] Similar to the ways in which nineteenth-century Shaker eldress Rebecca Jackson called on and trusted her *inner wisdom* and spirit to guide her through the terrors of losing credibility as a preacher woman in her denomination and being forced to make a risky decision to leave her church, home, and family in order to resist patriarchy, so, too, does intrareligious dialogue take on a sacred sharing within.[40]

Celebrating the work of first-wave womanist religious scholars and building on the methodologies articulated by the second wave, one of the primary hallmarks of third-wave womanist scholarship is the expansion of comparative religious and interreligious dialogue featuring the religiously pluralistic perspectives embodied by women of African descent across the globe.[41] Interfaith womanism acknowledges the wide variety of religious orientations, lifesystems, and spiritualities practiced by women of African descent or others who identify as womanist in their pursuit of justice work. Methods emerging from interreligious womanism explore the interreligious landscape of African diasporic religious traditions and use comparative religious and interfaith approaches while reflecting on issues of social justice (racial, gender, sexual, earth, economic). In addition, interfaith womanist approaches give special attention to developing interdisciplinary methods to find ethical imperatives for justice that exist in a variety of religious and spiritual practices, examining the impact of globalization and links across the African diaspora as well as identifying strategies of justice keeping and peacebuilding.

---

[39] Harris, *Gifts of Virtue*, 118–19.

[40] This might also be connected to Howard Thurman's idea of the inward journey. Howard Thurman, *The Inward Journey: Meditations on the Spiritual Quest* (New York: Harper and Row, 1961).

[41] For more on distinctions between the waves in womanist thought, see Harris, *Gifts of Virtue*.

The expansive nature of the term *womanist* and its reference to black women's spirituality is read positively by more and more scholars and in the works of Townes[42] and others. In widening womanist discourse, the emphasis on dialogue and inner dialogue continue to be central components of womanist interfaith and interreligious dialogue. The web-like openness of the definition of *womanist* was written by Walker to have "more room in it for changes,"[43] thus allowing womanist spirituality to take on a more fluid characteristic and not be burdened by ties to particular religious doctrine or dogma. This freedom of black women to express their spirituality in a variety of ways has become a foundation of womanist religious thought and a crucial point from which to argue against the systems of patriarchy, sexism, classism, racism, homophobia, and anthropocentrism in society and religions. Womanist interfaith dialogue helps women of African descent come to voice and offer reverence to Spirit in ways that clearly identify womanist wisdom, mutuality, inner sanctity, freedom, and community as values worth sharing.

---

[42] Emilie M. Townes, *In a Blaze of Glory: Womanist Spirituality as Social Witness* (Nashville, TN: Abingdon Press, 1995).

[43] See Walker, "Audre's Voice," 80.

CHAPTER SIX

Taking Action for Earth Justice: Teaching Ecowomanism

The image of live black women's bodies stretched along roads in North Carolina in order to block dump trucks from carrying toxic soil into their neighborhoods and destroying their gardens stays with me.[1] In his essay "Whose Earth Is It Anyway?"[2] James Cone reminds us of this brave band of black churchwomen who, in 1982, began a protest against soil contamination in Warren County that would attract thousands to the streets and land hundreds in jail. While jail time is familiar to those familiar with justice movements in the South, fighting for justice often has a cost. Holding up the banner for racial, economic, gender, sexual, and earth justice is a complex job that can leave marks—even in the college classroom.

---

[1] This chapter is a revised version of my essay, Melanie L. Harris, "Teaching toward Ecojustice: Integrating Womanist Justice and Environmental Concern in the Classroom," Spotlight on Theology Education, American Academy of Religion, March 2013, http://rsn.aarweb.org/ spotlight-on/theo-ed/environemental-justice/teaching-toward-ecojustice-integrating-womanist-justice-and-environmental-concern.

[2] James H. Cone, "Whose Earth Is It Anyway?" *Sojourners* (July 2007).

Raising awareness of environmental concerns in the midst of other more human-to-human-related justice issues among students in Texas can be a challenge. It is a state whose dependence on fossil fuels is announced proudly by consumerist practices of buying and driving large trucks, and in a state that has a legacy of wealth emerging from the depth of the ground up through oil wells, practical strategies for environmental sustainability aren't always accepted. Fracking and other drilling systems used to attain natural gas are not unfamiliar in a culture that celebrates these as new waves of technology helping to put many unemployed people back to work and finding ways to make entire communities comfortable, even in a bad economy. Still, there are recycling bins on campus. And student groups have launched their critiques to rally voices to speak out against overwatering the school's lawn. There is an impressive bike-and-ride program, but like most colleges and universities around the country, the students, faculty, and staff could do more toward environmental sustainability on campus and beyond.

Almost hearing the strong-lunged voices of those black churchwomen singing out songs of justice from the pages of Cone's essay, as a professor of ethics, African American religion, and environmental justice, what also comes to mind as I teach students to critically read this work is how to help them understand the connections between racial, economic, gender, sexual, and earth justice. As if digging deep into this very scene of protest in the essay, I encourage students to probe more deeply into the ethical questions posed by the hypothetical bystanders looking at those black churchwomen. "The civil rights movement is over. So why this act for justice now?" "What in the world are these black churchwomen doing out here protesting violence against the earth when they could be standing up for gender equality, women's rights, an end to mass incarceration, more peaceful conditions for women and children on the planet, or greater racial, sexual and economic justice?"

All of these issues are of course important to black women living on and with the earth. And from a womanist perspective that engages an interdisciplinary approach toward lifting up women's voices, theological inquiries, and concerns, all of these coincide with a womanist tenet: "commitment to survival and wholeness" expressed by Alice Walker in her definition of *womanist*.[3] Most students know the film *The Color Purple* directed by Steven Spielberg, or have heard about the Broadway production produced by Oprah Winfrey. What they often don't realize is that the Pulitzer Prize–winning novel is only one gem among many. Walker writes in a variety of genres, including as a human rights, social justice, and environmental activist. The *womanist* definition itself, recorded by Walker in her first collection of nonfiction books, *In Search of Our Mothers' Gardens*, actually gave birth to a movement in religion and theological discourse. In the 1980s, as African American women scholars and other woman scholars of color came to appreciate tripartite race, class, and gender analysis, many adopted the four-part definition as a theoretical framework to advance and validate their theological voices and concerns. In addition to racial justice, so pointedly articulated in the work of liberation theologians, and gender, economic, and sexual justice explained by feminist theorists, womanism emerged as a perspective that examined these justice issues in conversation with actual everyday life experiences of women of African descent living with and across the planet.

For womanists, surviving (thriving) and wholeness on the planet doesn't just refer to human-to-human encounters. It also means engaging and accepting the earth as community. Influenced in part by an African cosmological perspective that argues the interconnectedness of all beings in creation and emphasizes a connection between the natural environment, human life, and spiritual realm(s), many womanist perspectives embody a worldview that is inclusive of a moral imperative for earth justice. Furthermore, similar to reflections made by many writers in the black women's literary movement, there is a unique connection made between the treatment of

---

[3] Alice Walker, *In Search of Our Mothers' Gardens: Womanist Prose* (New York: Harcourt Brace Jovanovich, 1983), xi.

the bodies of enslaved black women in America (and beyond) and the harsh treatment of the body of the earth.

No one points this out more than womanist theologian, poet, and scholar Delores S. Williams. In her essay "Sin, Nature and Black Women's Bodies," she explains that there is a "relation between the defilement of earth's body, and the devilment of black women's bodies." She argues that the logic of domination, patriarchy, and a culture of violence against the feminine systematically "beat down" on the bodies, souls, and minds of black women and upon the earth. Drawing a parallel between strip-mining and the constant rape and sexual violence enacted upon the bodies of enslaved black women, Williams boldly asserts that the sin of defilement "manifest itself in human attacks upon creation so as to ravish, violate, and destroy creation: to exploit and control the production and reproduction capacities of nature, to destroy the unity in nature's placements, to obliterate the spirit of the created."[4] Developing a base for an ecowomanist perspective then, Williams's use of theological language to point to the parallel and systematic sin of oppression against black women and the earth is important to detecting cases of environmental racism. The bodies of black women and the body of the earth are deeply connected for ecowomanism, and, as such, the justice concerns of black women, emerging from their own bodily, historical, and social identities as having racialized, gendered, and historically economically valued bodies and identities, matters to all aspects of justice, including earth justice.

An ecowomanist approach then is an approach to ethics that centers the reflections and moral imperatives of race, class, gender, and sexual justice along with justice concerns for and with the earth. It can also be defined as "an approach to environmental ethics that centers the perspectives, theo-ethical analysis, and life experiences of women of color, specifically

---

[4] Delores S. Williams, "Sin, Nature and Black Women's Bodies," in *Ecofeminism and the Sacred*, ed. Carol Adams, 24–29 (New York: Continuum, 1993).

women of African descent, giving voice to their views and solutions to environmental problems."[5] Still other ecowomanist scholars, such as Layli Maparyan, have defined ecowomanism as "a womanist approach to ecological and environmental issues predicated on the womanist triadic concern with human beings, nature, and the spirit world simultaneously."[6]

Using Williams's example, and introducing students to other case studies of environmental racism, is important work that helps students make interdisciplinary connections between ecology, theology, ethics, and religion. Another teaching strategy that highlights this connection for students is placing environmental ethicists' works, such as Larry Rasmussen's *Earth Community, Earth Ethics*,[7] in conversation with books by ecoliterary writers, such as Alice Walker's *The Color Purple*.[8] By doing this, reflections can be made that remind students that the earth is one small *dot* among a vast universe and that we humans are in fact siblings to a whole host of other planetary beings. It is not enough, I find, to teach students simply about scientific facts and climate change or global warming. Rather, when teaching environmental ethics to college students taking a religious class, or a course on environmental ethics, I try to point to the larger issues of sustainability and relationship with the planet to engage mythical and religious stories of origin, and to study strategies of earth justice.

The integration of race, class, gender, sexual justice, and environmental concern has a deep impact on environmental

---

[5] Melanie L. Harris, "Alice Walker and the Emergence of Ecowomanist Spirituality," in *Spirit and Nature: The Study of Christian Spirituality in a Time of Ecological Urgency*, ed. Timothy Hessell Robinson and Ray Maria McNamara, 224 (Eugene, OR: Pickwick, Princeton Theological Monograph Series, 2011).

[6] Layli Maparyan, *The Womanist Idea* (New York: Routledge, 2012), 278.

[7] Larry L. Rasmussen, *Earth Community, Earth Ethics* (Maryknoll, NY: Orbis Books, 1996).

[8] Alice Walker, *The Color Purple* (New York: Harcourt, 1982).

ethics and pushes back onto some of the most foundational premises and policy making that have shaped preservationist and conservationist approaches to caring for the planet. Ecological perspectives that don't take environmental racism into consideration lose ground in the environmental justice movement because they disconnect the movement from earth care and from other justice-related issues. Ecowomanist perspectives seek to connect justice issues. Teaching this perspective not only opens the door to awareness of environmental changes we can make now but also teaches how strategies of environmental sustainability can be practiced by students working to change the future. Other pedagogical strategies that are helpful to share are discussed below.

Pedagogical Exercise

Having studied the Earth Charter,[9] students embark on writing their own earth covenants. Working in small groups, students are presented with an assignment that allows them to name five important themes in earth-justice keeping, gleaned from the readings, and to answer the following questions as they reflect on what their own earth covenant can be.

Questions for reflection include the following:

- "When did I first discover nature?"
- "How does my own social location (race, class, gender, sexual orientation, age, geographical point of origin, and communal/historical memory) engage or highlight particular aspects of environmental concern for me?"
- "What is my relationship to/with the earth?"
- "What are some of my religious views, values, and beliefs about my relationship to nature?"

---

[9] "The Earth Charter," in *Eco-Justice—The Unfinished Journey*, ed. William E. Gibson, 275–84 (Albany: State University of New York Press, 2004), http://earthcharter.org/discover/the-earth-charter/.

Following this small group exercise, students are presented with the challenge of creating a one-sentence thesis, motto, phrase, ritual, or poem that best captures the essence of their covenant and themes in their conversation. This move from more theoretical understandings of concepts in earth justice to practical engagement enhances students' learning and presents a different learning style for students who learn easily through hands-on practice. The following ritual is presented as a model.

Ritual Example

Invite the learning community to gather in a space in nature. This could be a space outside the classroom on campus or in a nearby park. Consider a space where there is an obvious presence of nature such as a space where trees stand or the sky is openly visible. Invite participants to *feel* or *touch* the earth. This can be done by inviting students to take their shoes off and walk barefoot on the grass, gather around and feel the trunk of a tree, study a fallen leaf, or close their eyes and be intentional about listening for winds or feeling gentle breezes. Once each participant has the opportunity to connect or commune with the earth, all are invited to gather in a circle. The following poem is read for reflection:

> *You are deeply rooted in the Earth.*
> *Her Amazing Grace flows through you.*
> *Her Divine Breath breathes through you.*
> *As wide as rivers run, and as far as oceans go—you are*
> *   deeply one with Earth Community.*
> *You are rooted in the Earth, and Earth is rooted in you.*

After a quiet moment of reflection, students are invited to dialogue in pairs to discuss how their own religious perspective, social location, and sense of environmental connection are made evident, or not, through the poem.

Litany

Coming back into a circle, the following three-step litany closes the ritual. As they speak the words below, students are first asked to recall particular themes they have noticed in their readings and how their own social location connects to a particular theme in ecojustice. Second, students are invited to speak these words to each other as they practice a deep embodiment of respect and value of each other or other *earthlings*, as Alice Walker calls us—beings all connected in the earth community. Third, students are asked to visualize or *commune* with nature while repeating the following:

> *I honor you.*
> *I honor the Earth.*
> *And I happily join you in the moves toward earth justice.*
> *I honor you.*
> *I honor the Earth.*
> *And I happily join you in the moves toward earth justice.*

CHAPTER SEVEN

Ecowomanism and Ecological Reparations

This chapter engages one primary question: in light of the significant contributions and templates for social justice organizing that have emerged from the Black Lives Matter movement, are there specific antiracist reparations paradigms that can be translated for ecological reparations work? In order to answer the larger question, I will focus on explaining what ecological reparations are from an ecowomanist perspective.[1]

Ecowomanism

Let us first circle back to a definition repeated several times in this volume: *Ecowomanism* is critical reflection, contemplation, and praxis-oriented study of environmental justice from the perspectives of women of color and particularly women of African descent. It links a social justice agenda with ecojustice, recognizing the parallel oppressions that women of color have often

---

[1] This essay is a revised version of my essay "Ecowomanism and Ecological Reparations," in *Wiley-Blackwell Companion to Religion and Ecology*, ed. John Hart (Hoboken, NJ: Wiley Blackwell, forthcoming).

survived when confronting racism, classism, sexism, heterosexism, and *similar* oppressions that the earth is facing through environmental degradation. While debatably anthropocentric in its focus, ecowomanism unashamedly lifts the lives of these women of color, as a starting point to reflect on climate justice, in part because of the historical and paradoxical connection that these women have with the earth.[2]

At the same time that conceptualizing the unique connections women have with the planet as mother, or the feminization of the planet, can serve as a connecting point to the lives of women, there is also an eerie familiarity to the structural nature of violence that the earth has faced (ecoviolence) and the structural forms of violence that black women have faced historically. For example, as womanist theologian Delores Williams points out in her constructive essay "Sin, Nature and Black Women's Bodies,"[3] during slavery (and since), black women's bodies were seen as property by white slave owners. Black women were not seen as fully human. When we compare the structural violence that ravaged the lives and raped the wombs of black women for the sake of a slave master's sexual gratification and compare this with the agricultural practices of overproducing cotton in the South (prior to the development of the cotton gin), for the sake of a profit, thus robbing the soil of nutrients in Mississippi and causing soil erosion in Alabama, we see the connection between violence against black women and violence toward the earth. In making these comparisons, an environmental justice paradigm, linking social justice to earth justice, becomes central when crafting climate solutions and raising consciousness about ecological reparations.

---

[2] Kimberly N. Ruffin, *Black on Earth: African American Ecoliterary Traditions* (Athens: University of Georgia Press, 2010).

[3] Delores S. Williams, "Sin, Nature and Black Women's Bodies," in *Ecofeminism and the Sacred*, ed. Carol Adams, 24–29 (New York: Continuum, 1993).

Ecowomanism and Ecological Reparations

In entering this conversation about ecological reparations, I am using an ecowomanist methodology that lifts up the work, lives, and scholarship of black women in the environmental justice movement. The method adopts womanist race–class–gender intersectional analysis and features a seven-step process, including

1. honoring womanist experience;
2. reflecting on womanist experience;
3. applying womanist intersectional analysis;
4. critically examining African and African American environmental religion, history, and tradition;
5. engaging transformation;
6. sharing dialogue; and
7. taking action for earth justice.

For the purpose of this chapter, it is helpful to explain how the method opens up to a larger emphasis on the prophetic wisdom of ecowomanism. In keeping with a third-wave approach, I enter into this conversation rooted to a deep sense of justice and open to using interdisciplinary methodologies. Who are my conversation partners? Those in the wider field of environmental ethics, religion, gender, peacebuilding, and ecology; activists working across the planet to raise awareness about climate change; brown and black communities waking up to the realities of the impacts of climate change on their bodies; and antiracist activists and scholars wrestling with racial reconciliation. All or many of these partners point to faith-inspired ethics (Christian social ethics) that insist that repair and repentance are still priorities in the work of justice. That is, it is *not* OK to simply dialogue our way around racism and environmental racism; at some point, if true transformation is to take place, a true apology must be offered, a change must be made, and we must acknowledge that the greed and pride that are woven into our white supremacist, overconsuming society has caused historical pain (trauma) and evidence of internalized oppressions —and, in too many instances, snuffed out the beauty of life with shots of racial and ecological violence.

Ecological Reparations

Ecological reparations center on repairing ecological violence and recognizing the logic of domination at play in ecocide and genocide—racial, gender, and sexual violence, and ecological violence. As Jennifer Harvey reminds us in her book *Dear White Christians*, there is something eerily familiar about the systemic ways in which white settlers justified *stealing* the lands of Native peoples throughout North America, based on their imperialist and colonialist claims and the *dominion biblical hermeneutic* used to interpret God's direction in Genesis 1:26 for (certain) humans to "have dominion and subdue the earth."[4] There is a connection, Harvey argues, between the white supremacy at work in the colonization of Native peoples and the Christianity that allowed them to dehumanize people and objectify the earth—all the while going to church and singing praises to God. As Native scholar Winona LaDuke in her book *All Our Relations: Native Struggles for Land and Life*, has claimed, the colonizing of peoples is interwoven with a mind-set that the earth itself can be commodified. In this thinking, *ecocide and genocide go hand in hand.*[5]

Ecological reparations face this truth. To repair acts of violence against Native peoples, and enslaved (or free) African women, we must interrogate the white supremacist mind-set and logic of domination that sits at the root of these structural forms of violence while seeing the impact that this logic of domination also has on the earth.

---

[4] Jennifer Harvey, *Dear White Christians: For Those Still Longing for Racial Reconciliation* (Grand Rapids: Eerdmans, 2014), 175.

[5] Winona LaDuke, *All Our Relations: Native Struggles for Land and Life* (Cambridge, MA: South End Press, 1999).

In addition to pricking consciousness, ecological reparations also dismantle white supremacy and colonial ecology by reshaping the traditional theoretical frames used in the discourse by reasserting values of interconnectedness and interdependence. In the words of Robin Morris Collins and Robert Collins, ecological reparations recognize that "the urgency of the need to repair the most impacted places on earth is based not simply on claims for justice, but on recognition of the common dependence of all living things on heavily affected living systems."[6] That is, in addition to recognizing the links between social justice and earth justice, ecological reparations problematize some of the frames of environmentalism, acknowledge the impact of colonial ecology, and replace dualistic understandings that divide the earth from the heavens, for example, with a more fluid frame that values interconnectedness and interdependence.

Reimagining Theology: Ecowomanist Analysis and the Challenge of Reshaping Dualistic Theological Frames

According to an ecowomanist vision, the values of interconnectedness and interdependence that serve as a new base for shaping ecological reparations emerge by validating African, indigenous, and fourth-world cultural perspectives. In the previous chapters I have argued that by honoring the African cosmological frameworks embedded within many African American approaches to ecological justice, one can more clearly see a deep devotion to the earth, and justification for earth care. However, it should not be assumed that a return to African cosmology happens in all African American faith communities or lives in all black liberation theologies that are trying more deeply to commit themselves to environmental justice.

---

[6] Robin Morris Collins and Robert Collins, "Environmental Reparations," in *The Quest for Environmental Justice: Human Rights and the Politics of Pollution*, ed. Robert D. Bullard, 217 (San Francisco: Sierra Club, 2005).

Challenges: Breaking the Addiction to Dualisms in Western Thought

While African cosmology suggests a fluidlike relationship between human, divine (spirit), and nature (earthly) realms, it is important to note the dangerous hierarchical dualisms that function normatively in Christian and Western thought. These, which can often be found in black Christian churches, can separate the earth from the divine realm. In dualisms, such as heaven vs. earth, spirit vs. body, and male vs. female, we see that instead of interconnections between the realms, a separation takes place that places one realm (heaven) over the other. When engaging religion, gender, and the earth, this kind of hierarchical dualism can be quite problematic. In theologies, for example, that discount the role of women in the church, one often finds this kind of dualism (male vs. female), whereby the man is placed in hierarchal relationship over the woman. Tracing this logic from human-to-human relationships to human-to-nonhuman relationships, it is easy to see ways in which the same logic of domination, which suggests the feminine be devalued within her own tradition, is the same logic of domination that suggests the earth be devalued. This challenge of hierarchal dualisms is taken up by many ecofeminist scholars and ecowomanist scholars, which adds to the discussion that the relationship that women of African descent have with the earth is paradoxical. At the same time that women have been dehumanized and devalued, and in some cases theologically forbidden from having an equal voice in church and society, scholars also note how women's connection with the earth is sacred. For example, a parallel is often drawn between an image of a woman as creator (creative producer of ideas, thoughts, ethical systems, agency, communities, children, godchildren, adopted children, neighborhood children, space, food, etc.) and the earth as a *mother* who also creates.

An African cosmology and principle of interconnectedness counters Western, Platonist, dualistic views depicting the earth and nature as separate and apart from the human realm. This is particularly important to note in the case of ecowomanism—for as we have heard, this Platonist dualism functions at a conceptual root in the theologies of many spirituals, blues songs, and hymns. Just recall for a moment the lyrics of the spiritual "A City Called Heaven":

> I am a poor pilgrim of sorrow, I'm left in this whole wide world alone. I have no hope for tomorrow, but I'm trying to make heaven my home. Sometimes I am tossed and driven, Lord. Sometimes, I don't know which way to roam. But I heard of a city called heaven, I'm striving to make heaven my home.[7]

The theology woven in the lyrics of the song connotes a strong separation between the world, a land of slavery, hard laborious connection to the land, and sorrow—and the place called heaven, in which a person has ultimate rest, peace, and freedom from oppression.

Instead of this Platonist dualism, African cosmologies present a more holistic perspective for religious perspectives about the earth, in which the realms of nature (the earth), humanity, divinity, and the spirit are interconnected. Black religious ethicist Peter J. Paris describes this rationality by naming each of the realms as "ontologically united and hence interdependent."[8]

The interdependence and interconnection that Paris explains as paramount in African cosmology and evident in some black liberation theology also establishes a common moral discourse or ethical worldview about the importance of rationality shared among African diasporic peoples around the earth. It also undergirds the ethical imperative for earth justice in many African American communities of faith.

---

[7] Hall Johnson, *A City Called Heaven, Negro Spiritual* (New York: Robbins Music, 1930).

[8] Peter J. Paris, *The Spirituality of African Peoples: The Search for a Common Moral Landscape* (Minneapolis: Fortress Press, 1995).

Honoring Complexity

As important as it is to return to African cosmological roots, it is naïve to think that an embrace of the *African nature* or *African cosmology* within these African American religious traditions (be they influenced by Christianity, Yoruba, or Candomblé) is without complexity. As Edward Antonio reminds us in his essay "Ecology as Experience in African Indigenous Religions,"[9] we must be wise enough to recognize the politics involved in colonial ecologies and carefully problematize any move to assume that a return to the *African* will somehow save the planet. In fact, the political and social construction of what it means to be *African* or *indigenous* has to be examined in environmental studies. We must use postcolonial analysis, even as we lift up African cosmologies, as an important starting point for conversations about environmental justice. The politics of colonial ecology must also be confronted in the work and vision of ecological reparations.

Ecological reparations construct a reparative framework that recognizes links between inequalities, the reality of globalization, the push for justice, and the urgency of climate change. Ecological reparations recognize that while nature is not concerned with the politics of environmental policy, the reality is that mainstream environmentalism often masks its implicit bias against communities of color, all the while trying to protect the earth and promote sustainability. An ecowomanist perspective helps us observe these connections on how they can contribute new solutions to climate change as well as be honest about where we really are. It invites us to consider the words of environmental scholars Collins and Collins, "Racism is real and has consequences on the environment," and

---

[9] Edward P. Antonio, "Ecology as Experience in African Indigenous Religions," in *Living Stones in the Household of God: The Legacy and Future of Black Theology*, ed. Linda E. Thomas, 146–57 (Minneapolis: Fortress Press, 2003).

in an age of police brutality against black and brown women and men, ecowomanism helps point out that what we are witnessing with the rise in racial violence, which the Black Lives Matter movement is trying to shed light on, is a rise in white anxiety about shifting global economics, changing racial demographics, and power. Collins and Collins explain the phenomenon, writing, "Environmentalism masks an unconscious racism that threatens to replicate racist outcomes even without conscious intent."[10] From an ecowomanist perspective, this truth is acknowledged: fear + white supremacy = racial and ecological violence.

As aptly noted by environmental ethicist Dan Spencer in response to Emilie M. Townes's presentation engaging on race, Ferguson, and democracy in 2015 at the American Academy of Religion, there is a link between white anxiety about economic loss and displacement of power, and the rise in racial violence against African Americans, Latinos, and other peoples of color in America right now. Almost echoing the disappointment that Martin Luther King Jr. expressed having when reflecting on the slow movement of the white moderate as recorded in his "Letter from a Birmingham Jail," today ecowomanists, and environmental activists from communities of color all over the world have pulled at the long coattails of traditional environmentalists and asked, *What do you say about the connections between ecocide and the genocide of Native and indigenous peoples? What say you about the legacy of slavery and the dehumanization of millions of people for the sake of building a base for a capitalistic society, and what say you about these peoples' connection with the earth?*

Environmental reparations are multilayered, building on a "framework for a reparative, restorative environmental policy based on justice first, then sustainability."[11] However, rather

---

[10] Collins and Collins, "Environmental Reparations," 209–21.
[11] Ibid., 209.

than stopping there, we must go further. We must engage movements like Black Lives Matter, and the frameworks and templates that they and others are using to dismantle white supremacy, and engage ecological reparations because social justice is earth justice.

Liberating Earth and Ecowomanism

As I have tried to make clear throughout this book, the ecowomanist approach is an interdisciplinary one in that it often builds on historical reflections of and by these women and links social justice issues, including gender, economic, racial, and sexual justice, to issues of ecological justice. This link between social justice and ecological justice is one of the marks of an ecowomanist lens. Pointing to parallel oppressions suffered by enslaved African women whose bodies were raped and violated for the purpose of breeding slaves during the history of American slavery, and the similar ways in which the body of the earth, including mountains, rivers, and farming fields, have been used and overused for economic gain and resource, ecowomanism claims that the same logic of domination that functioned as a theoretical underpinning for the transatlantic slave trade (and other forms of systemic oppression) is the same logic of domination at work in cases of ecological violence and control.[1]

Because ecowomanist approaches are often influenced by African, Asian, indigenous, Native, and fourth-world cultural

---

[1] Melanie L. Harris, "Ecowomanism: An Introduction," *Worldviews: Global Religions, Culture, and Ecology* 20, no. 1 (2016): 5–14.

and religious perspectives and worldviews, they place significant value on the interconnection between human, spiritual, and natural realms.[2] In many African religious traditional cosmologies, for example, there is an ancestral link between living humans, nature, and the spiritual realms. Whether acknowledged through offerings given in the name of familiar ancestors or deities, honoring the ancestors can sometimes be manifested in one's moral commitment to also honoring the earth.[3] While some critics will argue that a false assumption has been made when suggesting that all African religious traditions have an embedded moral commitment to ecological justice within them, or that practitioners necessarily abide by a moral code to care for the earth, it is the case that in contrast to most Western ideologies, African cosmologies generally maintain a connection between what social theorist Émile Durkheim called the sacred and the profane. Reflective of what religious historian Charles E. Long recognizes is unique about African and African American religious worldviews, a connection between the sacred and the profane, ecowomanist approaches also recognize all of life as sacred.[4] This includes an embrace of the mystical and the mysterious and an understanding of the interconnections of divine, ancestral, and human realms. Ecowomanism also embodies values that suggest all beings have innate worth and dignity.

Ecowomanism is inherently interdisciplinary and inter-religious, but when foregrounding the religious and spiritual aspects of ecowomanism, three questions serve as entry points

---

[2] Layli Maparyan, *The Womanist Idea* (New York: Routledge, 2012), 278–82.

[3] Edward P. Antonio, "Ecology as Experience in African Indigenous Religions," in *Living Stones in the Household of God: The Legacy and Future of Black Theology*, ed. Linda E. Thomas, 146–57 (Minneapolis: Fortress Press, 2003).

[4] Charles Long, *Significations: Signs, Symbols and Images in the Interpretation of Religion*, 2nd ed. (Boulder, CO: Davis Group Publishers, 1999).

into the dialogue: (1) What is the relationship between humans and the earth? (2) What do these creation stories, narratives, or interpretations of sacred religious teachings and texts suggest about the ethics of how we (humans) ought to be in relationship with the earth? (3) In light of the urgency of the ecological crisis and the impact of climate change on communities that are more vulnerable in our society, what might religious perspectives on environmental justice also say about caring for *the least of these* or communities that have been marginalized as a result of colonialism, racism, and other alienating oppressions?

The latter question serves as a valuable reflection question at the end of this book on ecowomanist discourse. Emerging out of the womanist tradition, ecowomanism focuses on justice. It also highlights the unique sociological, ethical, moral, religious, cultural, and historical contributions that African and African American women throughout the diaspora have made to the environmental movement. As such, ecowomanism is inherently interdisciplinary, interreligious, and intentional about making global links bridging the perspectives of African and African American women together. Another distinctive mark of ecowomanism is that like womanist religious thought and womanist discourse more broadly, there is a commitment to both theory and praxis. That is, theoretical foundations in the discourse rely on actual real-lived praxis and everyday experiences of women of color and especially women of African descent. This attention to the *everydayness* of African and African American women's perspectives is articulated well by womanist scholar and social ethicist Emilie M. Townes. In the final pages of her book *Womanist Ethics and the Cultural Production of Evil*, she writes that ethics from a womanist lens involves critical reflection on the "everydayness of moral acts."[5] As her poetic verse-critical prose states, this means reflection on

---

[5] Emilie M. Townes, *Womanist Ethics and the Cultural Production of Evil* (New York: Palgrave Macmillan, 2006), 164.

> *the everydayness of listening closely when folks talk or don't talk to hear what they are saying;*
> *the everydayness of taking some time, however short or long, to refresh ourselves through prayer and meditation;*
> *the everydayness of speaking to folks and actually meaning whatever it is that is coming out of our mouths; the everydayness of being a presence in people's lives. . . .*[6]

Womanist theory emerges out of this reflection on the practical, everyday ethical decisions, embodiment of religious and spiritual beliefs, and sociopolitical actions that inform African and African American women's lives and stories of survival and thriving, in spite of facing constant threat and multiple oppressions.

Whether by examining the slave narratives of Harriet Jacobs or the writings of Sojourner Truth, or reflecting on the moral courage and stamina of Fannie Lou Hamer throughout the era of Jim and Jane Crow in America, or taking seriously the protest cries today of Black Lives Matter in an era of racist police brutality, womanist critique and ethical reflection consider African and African American women's voices, theories, and practices valid forms of epistemology. Similarly, ecowomanism points to the work, religious lens, and values of women scholars and activists of African descent whose work, whether through the green belt movement or in the food deserts of South Dallas, contributes solutions to the environmental crisis we are living in. Other questions that ecowomanism addresses include the following: How have women of African descent survived multiple and layered oppressions throughout history, and what are the forms of spirituality and religion that may have informed their survival? What is unique about the healing practices of these women that have assisted other women and their communities to name, survive, and

---

[6] Ibid.

thrive in spite of facing a constant barrage of environmental health hazards? How have the religious and spiritual insights, practices, and worldviews engaging the environment helped to shed light on how religious practices might bring about healing of the earth? This is the work of justice, and the focus of ecowomanism.

Index

157